P9-CAM-163

Praise for *If the Battle is Over Why Am I Still in Uniform?*

Brenda is living proof of the indomitable human spirit that lives in all of us. Her story is incredibly moving. She draws you in from the very first page and leaves you wanting more. She is truly blessed with the gift of humor to encourage and inspire others. Cancer is no match for this woman!

> —Rolf Benirschke, Former Place Kicker for the
> San Diego Chargers, author of *Alive and Kicking* and
> *Great Comebacks from Ostomy Surgery.*

We read this book as part of our employee education book club program. Through Brenda's sharing, we became closer to our customer's needs.

> —Mary Benhardus, Handi Medical Supply, St. Paul, MN.

She makes being a nurse worth it!

> —Metro Oncology Nurse Program.

This book is a "must-read" for every Medical Student on the Planet!

> —Roxanne B. Saylor, *Independent Publishing Review*

More Praise for
If the Battle is Over Why Am I Still in Uniform?

This energetic and insightful paperback chronicles first hand a
tumultuous battle with rectal cancer. As the title suggests, humor
was the weapon of choice to cope with such a devastating situation.

—Ian Settlemire, Editor for the *Ostomy Quarterly.*

Poignant, funny, gripping only begins to describe this story. Brenda
Elsagher opens her heart, sharing intimate details of her journey to
survive cancer. This book is an absolute must read for every doctor,
nurse, and any healthcare worker in between. It is a tangible reminder
that patients are not just a diagnosis; each one has their own very personal story.

—Reneé Wall Rongen, Speaker/Consultant, Author of *Grandy's
Quilt: A Gift For All Seasons.*

If the Battle is Over, Why am Still in Uniform? offers a personal
account of the rich life possible after ostomy surgery. This book is a
good learning tool for families and caregivers of ostomates as well as
the general public. As the leading company of ostomy supplies across
the world, we are delighted to share the educational pages we provided with you, the reader.

—Mark Kennedy, Senior Product Manager-Ostomy,
Hollister Incorporated

IF THE BATTLE IS OVER WHY AM I STILL IN UNIFORM?

Humor as a Survival Tactic to Combat Cancer

BRENDA ELSAGHER

Expert Publishing, Inc.

IF THE BATTLE IS OVER WHY AM I STILL IN UNIFORM?
© copyright 2003 by Brenda Elsagher. All rights reserved. No part of this book may be reproduced in any form whatsoever, by photography or xerography or by any other means, by broadcast or transmission, by translation into any kind of language, nor by recording electronically or otherwise, without permission in writing from the author, except by a reviewer, who may quote brief passages in critical articles or reviews.

ISBN 1-931945-06-3

Library of Congress Catalog Number: 2003108116

Illustrated by Deborah Pierce
Cover, Interior Design & Typesetting by Mori Studio

Printed in the United States of America

Second Printing: April 2004

07 06 05 04   5 4 3 2

Andover,
Minnesota

Expert Publishing, Inc.
14314 Thrush Street NW,
Andover, MN 55304-3330
1-877-755-4966
www.expertpublishinginc.com

For my parents, Eugene and Helen Elsen. Dad, my hero—the original funnyman, and Mom, the remarkable, extraordinary woman. Also for my steadfast loves, Bahgat, John, and Hannah, who make me laugh every day.

Contents

Foreword

Brenda Elsagher is my friend. She didn't start out that way. We first met in 1998 when she was merely another "double book" on my overly busy clinic schedule. Her concern that day was sore feet. She was three years removed from her colon cancer surgery, the Rear Admiral, and all that you will read about shortly.

Brenda and I, as patient and doctor, have coped through her subsequent surgeries and her daily health needs. She constantly amazes me with her wit, her insight, and her depth of character in dealing with the hassles of her illness and the medical system.

Many of you, in reading this book, will think about your colon in ways you never thought of before. Be sure you look in the back of the book for information on your colon and the cancer that is the second leading cause of cancer death in our country. Colorectal cancer attacks men and women alike, but you can fight back. You should know that colon cancer is easy to cure if caught early enough.

Brenda's cancer was caught early enough, and her story should inspire you to stop putting off your screening appointment with your doctor.

This book is a story with many aspects. It is very funny, sad, and even, at times, scary. For my colleagues and me it should be something even more. It should be a lesson, a nudge, even a slap in the face to never let us forget that we don't treat cancer; we treat people.

Brace yourself for you are about to embark on a reading experience that will make you laugh and cry out loud. At least it did me.

—*Douglas N. Hotvedt, M.D., HealthPartners Internal Medicine*

Acknowledgments

I have many people to thank for guiding me along the way. For my friend, Monica Sausen, who held the lantern–expecting nothing in return. Thank you for your gifts of time and energy and late night guffaws.

For the late Judy Delton who believed in me and tutored me in the few short months we had together, and for the writing class friends who took me under their wings.

A very grateful thanks for my friends and family. You took me to appointments, cleaned my house, prepared meals, watched my children, visited me, shared your stories, and kept my family and me in your thoughts. I learned to receive your gifts and you honored me with your reliable love.

Thank you to my Bible study friends who prayed for my family, this project, and me, from the beginning months of our time together. We've had fun; one of these days I might even learn something about the Bible.

Thank you to Hollister Incorporated, for their commitment to ostomates and their caregivers all over the world. They have shown their support through the second printing of this book.

To my new friends, Harry and Sharron Stockhausen at Expert Publishing. Thanks for sharing your knowledge with me.

Unforgettable thanks for all caregivers in the medical field who took care of me, especially the doctors and nurses of Health Partners who saved my life and soothed my spirits.

For colon cancer patients past whose treatments paved the way for me and for those people still in the struggle.

Be Kind—
Everyone you meet is fighting
a hard battle.

—John Watson

Chapter 1
Thirty-nine
and Holding

I knew my entire life that someday I would be speaking about something important. I never thought it would be about my rectum; actually, lack of a rectum. Over the years, I had spoken about hair styling,
church issues, and positive self-esteem, but this I suspected was finally
"my calling." I wondered if perhaps God had the wrong number.

On my 39th birthday, my friends and I decided to celebrate at a
comedy club, at the Mall of America in Minnesota. I secretly dreamed
of being a comedian since I was old enough to get into a club. Carol
Burnett's physical antics, Joan Rivers' self-deprecating routines, and
Whoopi Goldberg's edgy perspectives shaped my view of comedy. I
fantasized about appearing at ease in front of an audience, microphone in hand.

Insecurities kept me from acting on my dream.

*Is there enough excitement in my life to warrant good material?
Am I smart enough?*

Comedians appeared well read.

*I'm lucky if I have time to read the back of the Cap'n Crunch box
while I eat my cereal.*

Politics were a hot issue for comics.

*Our former governor was bald and used to wear a feather boa and
pink tights. Do I want to even go there?*

I put comedians on a pedestal and I was envious of their talent.
The jokes that produced grand belly laughs, but had elements of bit-
ter truth, were my favorite. Despite the risks that came with performing, I wanted to be up on stage. With no appreciation for how much
effort went into a five-minute performance, my fantasy lived on.

Perhaps it was the jumbo margarita or facing forty that gave me the bravado to claim, "I'm going to do that, for my 40th birthday, you'll see *me* up on stage."

My friends politely nodded their affirmations.

No sweat, I have a year to work on that goal.

Chapter 2

Burn, Baby, Burn

Over the years, as a hairstylist, I suffered from hemorrhoids and heard they came with the long hours standing on your feet. Since then I discovered that stylists were not exclusive members of the hemorrhoid club. From time to time I had occasional rectal bleeding, but nothing that concerned my doctors. I used Tucks and Preparation H and continued on with life as usual. Regular check ups produced nothing out of the ordinary.

In September 1995, I was dieting for the thousandth time, exercising regularly, and happily losing weight. Infrequently, I experienced violent cramps, which I attributed to additional fiber in my diet. An urgency to get to the bathroom however, was new and, at times, embarrassing. No surprise I was losing weight, I was running constantly to the toilet. My hemorrhoids flared up again and I contemplated asking the druggist for a bulk discount price on Tucks. There was a little blood in my stool, but no different from previous episodes. The burning sensation from the hemorrhoids typically went away in a couple of days, but this time my usual remedies weren't working. Even eating Godiva chocolates didn't help.

I barely had time to pay attention. Life was busy with my curious, wide-eyed, three-year-old daughter Hannah, and her big brother John, a sensitive, funny five-year-old. My husband Bahgat, a native of Egypt, and I had been married for six years. We lived in a suburban neighborhood complete with cul de sac. We both worked full-time; he worked in the computer industry and I worked as a hairstylist and owner of a busy full service salon. The pace of life was quick, at times stressful, and mostly fun while we played with our children. We created schedules that allowed one of us to be home with the children while the other worked. We didn't go out a lot, rarely traveled, and our big excitement was to host occasional dinner parties. The kids loved it when we watched *Barney* or *Power Rangers* with them or went for a walk in the neighborhood. Bahgat and I tried to enjoy a movie with a rating higher than "G" after the kids were in bed, but inevitably one of us fell asleep. We were living a contented family life.

My hemorrhoids continued to bother me.

It usually doesn't hurt like this. How long has this been going on? I bet I'm going to need a hemorrhoidectomy for sure. It never hurt this intensely before or lasted this long. What else can I do for some relief?

I wasn't comfortable standing, sitting, or laying. As I styled my client's hair, I half listened to her conversation because the pain distracted me. The last time I felt throbbing like this was in my thirtieth hour of labor with John. I hoped this wasn't an eight-pound hemorrhoid.

One evening as Bahgat and I made love I knew something was wrong. My insides felt sore, as if I had internal bruises. I was too uncomfortable to continue. Lovemaking had never been painful during previous hemorrhoid flare-ups. Now that my condition extended to our marital life, Bahgat made me promise to call the doctor.

I phoned the clinic the next morning and scheduled an appointment for the following week. The pain was relentless, without a moment's reprieve. We had a destination that was forty-five minutes from home, and I insisted on driving to distract me from the pain, but even that didn't work. I became anxious, almost hysterical. Bahgat suggested I take Ibuprofen. I was not used to taking any medication and the thought had never occurred to me.

Within fifteen minutes, the burning symptoms subsided into a dull ache that I tolerated easily. Reluctantly, I kept the appointment with my doctor. I was feeling sheepish because I had no pain, and I had my previous gynecological exam only five months before. I anticipated this visit with the doctor would lead to the hemorrhoidectomy talk.

Chapter 3
Bringing Up the Rear

The day of my appointment I apologized to my doctor, a good-natured family practitioner, for probably wasting his time.

"Since taking Ibuprofen," I explained, "I am quite comfortable."

"How much are you taking?" he asked.

"I have been taking four tablets at a time. I guess that's 800 milligrams."

"And how often are you taking them?"

"Three to four times a day. I'm afraid to quit taking them, though, in case the pain comes back. It was horrible."

After doing a slightly painful rectal examination, the doctor confirmed that I had a large hemorrhoid in need of treatment.

"Brenda, is it all right with you if I have the surgeon take a look at this? He happens to be in today and he has more experience than I in this area and can advise you better on what should be done. I'll go see if he has time."

Sure, why not? I'm laying here already—the more the merrier.

His colleague, the surgeon, was interested in seeing the nasty hemorrhoid and advised my doctor to move me to the procto room down the hall.

Older people always talk about proctos in hushed tones. What the heck do they do in the procto room anyway? Whatever it is, I hope they're not planning on doing it to me.

Upon entering the room, I noticed its unusual color—baby-poop green. No cheerfulness or attempt to make a patient feel relaxed in there. This was a place where they got down to business.

Entering shyly, an attractive, middle-aged nurse handed me a gown, and, without looking into my eyes, said the doctor would be in shortly.

A bold knock on the door, and I was facing a white-haired man who possessed an air of self-confidence. In his booming voice, he introduced himself to me and explained that he needed to do a vaginal and rectal exam. He proceeded without further pleasantries. After a quick visual and finger-probing exam, he informed me matter-of-factly, that I had a growth more serious than a hemorrhoid.

"This is either a tumor or cancer or something. It's much more than a hemorrhoid problem. I want to perform a biopsy today and get it to pathology to find out what kind of growth we have here."

He asked me a few embarrassing questions, "Did I have a fistula?"

What the hell is a fistula?

"Did I ever pass stool through my vagina?"

I answered back with a question, "Can you do that?"

I don't think I have ever done that. Wouldn't I know? Weird, why would he ask me that? I'm freaking out a little here.

As he snapped off his gloves, threw them in the garbage, and turned toward the door, he said, "The nurse will be in to give you an enema before the biopsy so I can visualize the growth clearly with a scope. We need to clean you out as much as possible."

Privately and much later I began to refer to the surgeon as "The Rear Admiral," but I was unnerved by my first interaction with this gruff, steely man. He left the room, and I was thankful for a few moments alone with my thoughts.

Geez, what a serious guy. No Mr. Friendly awards for him. What did he say about a tumor or cancer? This must be an unusual looking hemorrhoid to cause all this fuss. I'm sure they're being cautious over nothing. Luckily, we don't have cancer in my family. I'll probably end up having that darn hemorrhoidectomy. Ouch! The teasing I'll get from my family. I can hear them now tormenting me with perfect a—hole jokes.

The nurse knocked timidly and looked uncomfortable as she entered the room. I had the feeling I made her nervous. She handed me an enema kit and I began reading the directions on the box.

Noticing my confusion, she asked, "Haven't you ever done an enema?"

Not high on my list of priorities.

"No, can't say that I have."

She explained the procedure to me as she readied the room gathering sheets and unusual tools. Taking a rolling stainless steel stand, she began to place them neatly in a row and then covered them with a little blue paper towel.

I can see it comes in handy to have a bathroom adjacent to the procto room.

It didn't take long before the enema took effect. Luckily I had something to read. As I waited in the bathroom, I opened the newspaper and my eyes caught an article about a hairstylist who was working with cancer patients. Inspired by his mother, recently deceased from cancer, he fitted wigs for patients losing their hair as a result of cancer treatments.

Okay, if I have cancer I'll call this guy. I'll get a wig. I'll be fine.

I overheard the muffled loud voice of the surgeon and my family practitioner talking outside the door in the hall.

"I'm glad to fit her in, she's a very sick lady. The sooner the better."

Are they talking about me? I'm sick? I feel fine. I just have a pain in my butt. They must be talking about someone else.

All this attention was starting to scare me. The nurse came back to finish preparations for the biopsy.

Is it my imagination or is she purposely not looking at me? She knows something and can't look me in the face. It must be bad. She looks painfully uncomfortable.

As the surgeon was about to return, the nurse showed me where to kneel on the platform protruding from the table.

Concerned since previous surgery on both knees prevented me from kneeling for more than a few seconds, I asked, "How long will I have to kneel?"

"You don't kneel much at all. The table rotates forward electronically so there will be no pressure on your knees."

I knelt down as instructed and the table began to tilt. Soon I was laying flat and had to grab the table firmly, afraid I might slide to the floor as it tilted downward.

That nurse was right, no pressure on my knees. She forgot to mention the part about the blood rushing to my head.

As I thought about how humiliating it was to have the biggest part of my body sticking up in the air, the doctor came in ready to proceed. He inserted a rigid lighted tube, the proctoscope, which felt like it was three feet wide by seventeen feet long.

The pain was unbearable. I was afraid I'd pass out. I wanted to remain conscious so I decided to engage the doctor in a little light-hearted banter.

"Doctor, why do you think God put our rectums way back there? Why not on our hips or someplace easier to reach?"

The Rear Admiral didn't say anything.

Apparently he isn't into having a conversation. Well, maybe his hearing isn't that great. I feel better when I talk; I think I'll give it another shot.

"Doctor, that's kind of a gross job you've got there, isn't it?"

Without hesitation he responded, "It saves lives."

I sobered up quickly and wondered if he was talking about me. After a few moments of silence as he finished the exam he intoned a litany of advice,

"Don't drink alcohol."

"Don't eat spicy foods."

"Don't leave the country."

"Don't leave the clinic without seeing me in my office."

He gave me his home phone number and instructed me to call him day or night if I developed continuous bleeding. He left the room.

As I dressed I could barely button my blouse as my hands shook. Bahgat came into the room and asked why it was taking two hours. I told him the doctor said something about a tumor or cancer. Bahgat looked at me and said "Nooo."

Wanting to continue my denial, I echoed his "Nooo."

That day the whole family had come along to the clinic. Bahgat was there to have a mole removed from his forehead, John was having a culture for strep throat, and Hannah came along for the ride. We were all spending the day at the clinic. Some families go to the zoo.

Chapter 4
The Plan of Attack

Bahgat and I gathered our children and went across the hall into the surgeon's small office. The nurse cleared off one chair and brought another.

It's not cancer. I know he's going to tell me I need a hemorrhoidectomy. Must be a bad one. Damn.

Scared by all the attention, my breathing was shallow, and I was on the verge of tears. The room felt smaller with each passing moment. The kids sat on the floor enthralled by a troll doll wearing a little green scrub outfit. I was concerned they might damage it and hoped the doctor wasn't too attached to the troll in case it wasn't returned in the same condition. I wondered who gave it to him.

The Rear Admiral came into the room, sat down, and leaned as far back in his chair as possible, almost as if he wanted to get away from me.

He said, "There is no easy way to tell you this. Even without the biopsy results, I am almost one hundred percent sure you have carcinoma of the rectum."

I panicked, talked fast, and tried to hold back tears so I could ask the important questions.

"Is that cancer of the rectum? What does that mean? I don't know anyone who has had cancer of the rectum. I know a lot of people and I've never heard of anyone having cancer of the rectum. Don't you need your rectum?"

He pointed to a poster of the intestinal tract on the wall behind him and showed us where the tumor was located in the colon.

"Brenda, because of the location of this tumor you will have to have your rectum removed, part of your vaginal wall removed and reconstructed, a complete hysterectomy, and a permanent colostomy."

The way he said it so matter of fact sounded like he was dictating his grocery list to me.

"Do you understand what I am explaining to you?"

"I think so. It doesn't sound good."

"Eighty percent of the people diagnosed with colorectal cancer live past five years. We'll find out more as we go along."

A part of me started comprehending the horror of what he was saying. Imagining myself with a bag hanging off my stomach, I started crying and felt like I was falling apart. I couldn't concentrate well.

How does a reconstructed vagina work?

I cried and felt as if my spine was turning into jelly and liquefying into the chair. The next moment I felt as if part of me detached from this trauma and floated above to a corner of the room. Observing the scene below, I watched my children play with the troll and listened to the doctor explain the gruesome details to Bahgat and me. With worry on their faces, the kids turned to me as I sat crying in the chair.

The unconscious part of me took in the features of the room and studied the doctor's credentials on the wall. I watched Bahgat look at me with tenderness and disbelief at what he was hearing. I imagined the words "Everything will be okay" scrolling along the walls of the room as if posted on an electronic message board.

Suddenly, the two parts of myself merged as I fired questions at the surgeon.

"When you say colostomy, are you talking about the bag thing? You mean, forever?"

He nodded affirmatively.

"Will I have to have chemo and radiation too?" He explained that an oncologist would meet with me and determine that protocol.

I was angry and agitated.

I have eighteen clients tomorrow. My license tabs have to get renewed. I have to pick up our tickets for Egypt.

In exasperation I said, "I don't know you. I need to get another opinion before I have an operation like that."

He asserted in a slightly tense voice, "I have more than thirty years of experience in this field and I recognize this cancer. I suggest you wait seventy-two hours until we have the biopsy results before you make any other plans."

As I cried uncontrollably, my children sought my embrace. I gathered Hannah and John in my arms and scheduled an appointment in three days. Scribbling the return time down on a card, the clinic staff cast sympathetic glances our way and talked quietly amongst themselves. We walked slowly out the door.

Sometimes, you have to fight a battle more than once to win it.

—Margaret Thatcher

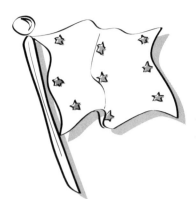

Chapter 5
I Want to Go AWOL

*I*n the parking lot we remembered we had driven two cars. Bahgat had crucial data for a pre-arranged overseas conference call at work. We decided he would go to the office and finish his project while I took the kids for a drive-thru dinner. Needing the moral support of my family, we agreed to meet later at my parents' home.

Through more tears, I planned my funeral as I drove. I recalled a conversation the previous week with Bahgat. We discussed funeral rituals in the Catholic faith and the options for Muslim burials in Minnesota. I had written a list of favorite songs to be sung at my funeral—"On Eagle's Wings," "Silent Night," "Were You There When They Crucified My Lord?" "America the Beautiful."

I guess I can scratch "Grow Old Along With Me" from my list.

Fresh on my mind was our friend, Terri, who lost her thirty-eight-year old husband to cancer a few months prior. Like us, they had two young children. I wondered if that conversation the week before foreshadowed our own experience.

By the time I got to my folks' house I felt exhausted and resigned to doom. Usually an optimist, I couldn't shake morose thoughts.

How will the kids and Bahgat handle my hair falling out? I don't want them to see me throwing up, listlessly lying around with my pajamas on and no energy to lift my babies into my arms. No other woman can mother them the way I do. They like it when I read to them in funny voices and when we pray together at night. I want to see my children grow up, to get excited with Hannah as she dresses for her first Sadie Hawkins dance or see John driving for the first time. The thought of not laughing with them about private jokes or exploring the fifty states together makes me crazy. Bahgat needs my teasing; he works too hard and takes life too seriously. I want to visit Paris with him. It took us too long to find each other. Damn it, I am not ready to say goodbye.

When my parents opened the door, they didn't seem surprised to see me. They explained Bahgat had called my sister, Shelly, who called my parents and business partners to relay the news.

Mom busied herself with helping John and Hannah at the table. Once the kids were settled, I relayed the news I had learned the last few hours. My father, who doubled as our financial planner, listened intently to what I was saying. Questions erupted from me like an over-flowing popcorn maker.

"Dad, do you think we have enough money in case I die? Would Bahgat be able to handle the finances alone? Do you think I should check my paperwork and make sure everything is in order? I don't even know what kind of life insurance we have on me. I bet it isn't enough."

He let me jabber awhile. Then calmly he said, "You know Brenda, you just might live."

I hadn't thought of that angle yet. That sounded good. I felt some-one had taken a warm blanket out of the oven and was slowly spread-ing it out on top of me.

I just might live. I like that. It's possible. Not everyone dies from cancer. I might live indeed.

I related a statistic mentioned at the clinic that eighty percent of people who have cancer of the rectum live five years. Mom and I understood it incorrectly. We misinterpreted the statistic to mean if I was lucky, I could live up to five years.

Soon I heard Mom calling my aunt, uncle, and siblings to join us. Mom couldn't stop crying and consoled herself with a Jack Daniels and 7-Up. I went for the brownies.

Aunt Betty and Uncle Don, my godparents, were the first relatives to arrive. We talked about October 2nd, being the anniversary of their eldest son's death. It was also my sister Laurie's birthday. Now it would also be known as the day I was diagnosed with cancer of the rectum. Bahgat finally arrived, and I felt better having him near me.

"Did you say you have colon cancer or cancer of the rectum?" asked Betty.

"I think they're the same. The doctor also called it colorectal cancer. He said the rectum is the lowest part of the colon. Let's face it. I have cancer of the a—hole."

Between phone calls coming in from the rest of the family and being the center of attention to the people present, I was getting tired of all the surveillance.

Why can't I have a more respectable cancer? One that isn't so disgusting to say, like cancer of the elbow. There she is, the one with cancer of the rectum.

I could picture my family's sphincter muscles tightening as I told them what would be happening to me. We discussed second opinions, work schedules, doctor's appointments, and pooping in a bag. Dad told me he heard that comedian Bob Hope had a colostomy. He also mentioned people we knew, people who lived through similar experiences and were leading average everyday lives. Eventually I got tired of crying, talking, and being the focal point of the family. I was anxious to put some of the day's emotion behind me and grateful to use Hannah and John's presence as a reason to depart. I had to go home and get my little ones to bed.

Chapter 6
Rectum is Such a Dignified Word

*T*he phone was ringing as I came through the door. It was Michele, a friend since Campfire Girls. News travels fast.

"You heard the news about me already?"

"Heard what news?"

Awkwardly I stammered out words that included cancer. Recognizing how people often associate cancer with death, I dreaded hearing her panic and fear.

"What can I do to help?"

"Call our friends and let them know for me. If they feel like praying, that wouldn't hurt either."

The next day I went to work, navigating through tears as I drove.

I better get a hold of myself, that's all I need–to be pulled over by the police.

"Ma'am, did you know you're driving erratically? What seems to be the problem?"

"No problem, Officer, I just have cancer of the a—hole."

My decision to go to work was rewarded as my co-workers arrived. No words were spoken. One stylist blew me a kiss as she walked by; another squeezed my hand, while a third paused to give me a quick hug.

Somehow, I was able to compose myself enough to get through each haircut. Many times I had consoled people who tearfully disclosed personal stories while sitting in my chair. I couldn't guarantee good work if I did the same. I imagined myself sobbing through bleary eyes, asking, "A little more off the sides?"

Fitting cancer into my calendar made me angry. I couldn't predict what my work days or hours would be. Cancer was not course work we ever studied in beauty school. I recalled the textbook's advice to be cautious discussing religion and politics, but cancer? "Acting in a Professional Manner in the Salon After Diagnosis of Cancer of the Rectum 101," was not offered.

A client called that afternoon. She requested I take a little more off the length. "Is it possible you could fit me in today? I want to go out of town, and I have a million things to do."

"I'm sorry. I am too booked up; how about next week?"

Exasperated, she said, "It shouldn't take you that long."

"Look, I was diagnosed with cancer of the a—hole yesterday. I am doing the best I can to fit everyone into my schedule while I figure out tests and stuff."

She got really quiet and stammered out, "It's okay; don't worry about it."

Two hours later flowers were delivered. I walked up to the desk to look at the card.

My first cancer flowers, this sucks.

Referring to my illness as cancer of the a—hole, my language reflected my exasperation. My sister, Shelly, a partner in the salon, overheard my conversations with clients.

"Brenda, couldn't you use the word rectum instead of a—hole— please?" she pleaded.

To say cancer of the rectum almost seemed dignified, and I didn't want to grant it that privilege.

Why am I so embarrassed? Why should I have shame about having a tumor in my rectum? Are people going to like me less because of where my tumor is located? Does any tumor have a politically correct location?

Eventually I decided there was no need to embarrass anyone else in this process. I resigned myself to rectum.

Chapter 7

Assembling the Troops

Seventy-two hours passed since we were at the clinic. I cried continuously the first day, but the second day, I didn't shed a tear. Instead, I laughed about everything. Anxious for the meeting with the doctor, I thought it was a good idea to bring reinforcements in case my mind wandered. Armed with my own private battalion, Bahgat, as my squad leader, and my mother as secretary of defense, we were ready to hear the biopsy results. Mom's job was to help me avoid misunderstandings about upcoming appointments. She scribbled constantly on her yellow legal pad, and Bahgat fired away with questions. I was educating myself on cancer of the rectum and preparing for the battle ahead.

Studying mating habits of Minnesota mosquitoes sounds more appealing.

"Your biopsy was positive; it is a malignant tumor."

The surgeon noted the tumor's location and described the surgery he needed to perform.

"Your rectum will have to be removed and your large intestine rerouted to an opening in your abdomen resulting in a permanent colostomy. You will need a total hysterectomy because we will need to remove and reconstruct the vaginal wall that shares the same location with the tumor for a safe cancer margin."

Now we have the battle plan.

The Rear Admiral said, "All that sounds bad, but actually, that's the good news."

My heart sank. I wondered how that could be the good news.

Excuse me? Good news is, "You have a beautiful baby boy," or "You've won the 10 million dollar jackpot," or "Take the day off today—with pay."

He continued, "If the cancer has spread to major organs or throughout your body we won't bother with the operation. We'll try to make you as comfortable as possible."

I had not thought of cancer spreading throughout my body. It became a defining moment. Fueled by fury, my whole attitude shifted during that brief, poignant, conversation.

They aren't giving up on me. I won't let them! Make me comfortable? I don't think so. I don't care if it hurts. I don't care if I have poop coming out of my stomach. I can live with that. There are a lot worse things than having a colostomy.

Emphatically, I instructed the doctor to make me well.

"I intend to dance at my children's weddings."

A smile came across his face for the first time.

"Good. We're going to do the best we can to make that happen."

Believing the Rear Admiral, I progressed from being mortified about having a colostomy to being proactive about my health. There was no room for being self-conscious about having cancer of the rectum, nor would anyone else's potential embarrassment shame me into silence. I would willingly take every test necessary and let people help me—whatever capacity was required. There would be little time for indulging in self-pity; I would endure what needed to be done. Living would be my priority, no doubt about it.

Now we have the mission objective. Time to face the battle.

"Will we still be able to visit Egypt in eight weeks?"

It was to be our first trip back to Bahgat's homeland with our children.

"It might be possible, depending on what is decided about chemotherapy or radiation with your oncologist."

Oncologist. I don't like that new word.

The surgeon walked me to the scheduling desk and set up a CAT scan for the following morning. I was warming up to this austere physician. Mom never liked him. She acted like he was personally responsible for my cancer. I reminded her, he was only the messenger.

Even so, I overheard her angrily telling my father later that day, "That doctor is such an a—hole."

My father replied, "Actually, Helen, he's an a—hole remover."

I lay in my bed and stared at the ceiling for what seemed like hours. I couldn't sleep that night, tossing and turning with worry. The CAT scan results would determine my future course of treatment. I turned to Bahgat, "What if it's in my liver? What am I going to do?"

Then almost getting hysterical I repeated, "Bahgat, what if it's in my liver?"

A master with puns, Bahgat said tenderly, "Oh, liver alone."

I groaned my response and within minutes I was fast asleep.

The next morning, on my way to the CAT scan, I narrowly missed a car entering the freeway. While waiting for my mother, I drank the first bottle of medicine required for the scan. Driving to the hospital, we had the difficult mother-daughter conversation.

I concentrated on my driving and stared straight ahead. I couldn't bear to look at her.

"Mom, I have been pretty happy most of my life. Hannah and John thrill me; it was the best thing I ever did having kids and aren't they beautiful? Bahgat's a good husband who loves me and works hard for us; he's the one who's going to need support. I am grateful to you and Dad for all the sacrifices you made for me. No matter what this test result is going to be, I want my quality of life to remain fun to the end. I count on you for that."

I asked for her promise. "Okay?"

She responded quietly, "Okay."

This was uncharted territory, the unimaginable death of a daughter before her mother. I avoided a pothole.

God forbid I get killed on the way to the hospital.

Some people face mortality by going out on three-day drinking binges, others max out their charge cards. I rebelled by being cavalier about wearing my seat belt. It was the warped way I took control of my life.

There goes tough Brenda. She's not putting her seat belt on today. She's decided to live dangerously now that she's been diagnosed with cancer. She's really testing fate now. Cancer and no seat belt, she's living on the edge.

At the CAT scan, I drank my second dose of chalky solution intended to provide a clear picture. The prep nurse told me about a patient and a cute young nurse who readied him for his test. He was in the tunnel-like machine for the time it takes the machine's recorder to say repeatedly, breathe in, breathe out, and hold your breath. When the test was completed and the patient was rolled out of the machine, he opened his eyes to see a much older nurse attending him.

"I knew I was in there awhile but I didn't think it was *that* long!"

I suspect they had seen lots of people sicker than me. Holding onto their words of encouragement, I left the room smiling.

The radiologist appeared to be barely out of medical school. The purpose of meeting with him was to determine if radiation would be most effective before or after surgery.

After his examination I asked, "What do you advise? Chemo, radiation, or surgery first?"

"Sometimes it helps to shrink the tumor before the operation."

"Is that what you recommend?"

"I can't make that decision. There is not enough data to tell you definitively that it should be done before the surgery."

"What are you saying, you can't tell me what to do?"

"You'll have to make that decision."

I was furious.

Wait a second. What do you mean, I'll have to make that decision? Aren't you the medical expert? If not, then what the hell am I doing here? Aren't you supposed to know more about radiation than me? I am a hairstylist. I didn't just ask you if you wanted your hair cut above your ear. I asked you for an opinion in your area of expertise. I don't know anything about chemo, radiation, or operations. Why can't you medical people decide what should be done first? How can I make this choice?

Instead I asked, "What would you do if I was your wife?"

He said there was no documentation to recommend one course of treatment over another. He would not take a stand, even after I approached him from all angles. He continued to repeat that I would have to make that decision after consultations with the remaining doctors. We were finished for the day and free to go home.

"I'm not leaving here without the results of my CAT scan."

He left Mom and me alone while he went to check the outcome of my test. Ever the faithful secretary, she took notes and asked hard questions while I took mini-vacations in my head. While I changed out of the hospital gown, we weighed the question of what should come first—chemo, radiation, or surgery.

Then my secretary said confidently, "It's just like buying a new couch. When you get it home, you've got to try it out in many positions around the room."

When my mother started likening treatment options to redecorating her living room, I questioned if it was time to get a new secretary. The stress was getting to both of us.

A short time later, the good news was delivered. No cancer in my major organs. Despite the encouraging results of the scan, I left with the most bothersome question still unanswered. Which treatment should come first—chemo, radiation, or surgery?

Chapter 8
Mine Eyes
Have Seen
Your Glory

Over the next ten days I saw eight different doctors and had eight vaginal and rectal exams. It seemed as though everything proceeded at a frantic pace. All along, I still had a business to maintain, clients who needed hair services, and young children who wanted dinner. The world did not stop because I was diagnosed with cancer.

I felt like I had been playing hide and seek with cancer and just got found. People would ask me if I ever thought, "Why me?" I'd have to say no. It was more like, "Why not me?" What would make me any less prone to getting cancer than someone else? Cancer isn't logical. It's crafty, unpredictable, and random.

I met with the oncologist, a tired looking man who seemed to carry the weight of the world on his shoulders. He had puppy-dog eyes, a gentle smile, and a relaxed, kind disposition. An essay about the importance of attitude and cheerleading affirmations was tacked up on the wall in his office.

"There are no specific guidelines on colorectal cancer as to the best protocol with one procedure outperforming another."

We discussed chemotherapy and radiation at great length.

"I wonder if you would be interested in being in a colon cancer study. If you agree to participate, the protocol of the study will determine whether you have surgery before or after chemotherapy and radiation. The decision will be out of your hands. You still need to talk with the doctor that will be doing the vaginal part of the surgery before you can make that decision."

"I heard a statistic that eighty per cent of colon cancer patients live up to five years, is that right?"

"Actually, colon cancer detected early through colonoscopy, is one of the most preventable cancers with a ninety percent survival rate past the standard benchmark of five years. After that time, they don't keep statistics on survival rates."

"Was mine detected early enough?"

"That is what we are finding out through all these tests, surgery will be important to test the lymph nodes as well."

Testing was a priority now and everything else revolved around that schedule. Hurry to this test then wait for results. I was probed and scanned in parts of my body I never thought of as photogenic. Each test had its own devastation. The anticipated humiliation and embarrassment was often the worst part of the procedure.

Various friends accompanied me to my tests so Bahgat could work or remain home with the kids. My nurturing friend, Sherry, was the first to bring a meal to my home when she heard of my diagnosis.

"I hope you like lasagna. I didn't know which you'd prefer, veggie or regular, so I just brought both."

The food was good but nothing compared to the love and attention she fed me.

Sherry came with me to many medical appointments, the first being the painful, awkward vaginal and rectal ultrasounds. She held me lovingly as I sobbed hard after each test before we moved on to the next. Sherry was amazed I could wrap up my tears in five-minute intervals. The magnitude of the tests always weighed heavily on my mind. Affording only a minimal indulgence in emotion, I didn't have time to fall apart. I had to stay focused on what needed to be done.

Many friends continued to call to offer help with the kids or give me rides to tests. My sister Laurie, who lived abroad in Japan, wrote emails wanting to help.

Brenda, I guess I could donate my vagina if you need it. Mine hasn't had much use lately. I prefer to keep my own rectum however. Love, Laurie

Among the tests required were a mammogram, chest x-ray, blood and urine analysis, and a colonoscopy. I dreaded the colonoscopy. I knew it was important, but the idea of a lighted garden hose up my rear end didn't thrill me, especially after experiencing the rigid sig-moidoscope in the doctor's office during the biopsy.

My friend since grade-school band, Corinne, drove me to the colonoscopy, which turned out to be the least painful of all the tests. The sedative worked its magic, similar to a triple Bacardi and Coke. The actual test was nothing compared to drinking the salty tasting liq-uid ironically named "GoLytely" in preparation. No question you're homebound during the twelve hours before the test. Purification of the bowels does not enhance social events. It's a definite book or TV night.

Accompanying me to other appointments was Michele, who always made me laugh. It was great that she could come along because I figured we would need levity for the dreaded discussion with the enterstomal therapist (ET).

The stylishly dressed ET nurse exuded confidence as she described her specialized training in caring for ostomies and wounds. It was obvious she had given this talk before because of the ease of her delivery. I was comfortable with her instantly.

She handed me literature that described the function of my colon. Prior to that time it was a part of my body I never thought about. Like my car or television, I didn't have to know how it worked as long as it ran well.

I listened as the nurse methodically explained what living with a colostomy would be like. She paused after each sentence to wait for my reaction. I thought that was odd but realized the scope of what she was telling me was so foreign, it would take awhile for me to fully grasp the information. As I asked more questions, she gave answers.

I innocently asked, "Where do the farts go?"

Calmly she responded, "In your pouch. Flatulence as well as stool is expelled into the colostomy pouch."

My resolve to not cry was shattered.

Poop and farts in a bag the rest of my life. I wonder how Bahgat will cope with this—will he still love me the same? I can't imagine making love with this thing attached to me.

We talked about sex. She mentioned that her husband was an ostomate, and their sex life was not at all affected by his ostomy. She assured me it would not be an issue for us as a couple over time.

Once the educational portion of the appointment was concluded, it was time to get tattooed for placement of the stoma, the external end of the colon that would be protruding from an opening in my abdomen. I sat, stood, and bent over to determine where the waistband of my slacks and the natural folds of my skin were located.

This is embarrassing. Standing up and sitting down to determine where my fat folds will fall. I hate this. I'm losing the privacy of my own body and it can't be helped. Finding the right spot is more important than how fat my stomach looks.

Having a flat surface that didn't interfere with clothing would make caring for the colostomy easier. She decided on a location and marked an X with purple ink at the site.

That is where the hole is going to be. My intestine is going to hang out of that X'd spot. Another place on my body I never cared about before. I'm sorry I haven't loved that spot more, now that it matters. I wish I hadn't taken it for granted.

The nurse gave Michele an informational video and literature to take home for me and we left. I got in Michele's car, cried for my self-imposed five-minute allocation and was late getting back to the salon. We tried to talk about anything but what we had just been through together; even Michele couldn't joke her way out of this one.

"Do you have to go back to work? Maybe we could go get a drink or dinner or something."

"Michele, no doubt I need several drinks, but I have a lot of appointments tonight, it's too difficult to cancel and reschedule them. I am not sure with all these tests when I have to take off work from day to day. I better just go back."

"Somebody could probably reschedule them for you, Brenda."

"Tempting as that is, Michele, it's such a hassle to ask anyone to do. I better go back to the salon. I am already thirty minutes late. Can I use your phone to call them and tell them I'm on my way in?"

"Sure, Brenda. After I drop you off, I think I'll go to your folks house and show them the literature and video about your colostomy so they can understand more about it too, okay?"

"I appreciate that, Michele, and thanks for coming with me today; another new experience to add to our list. Sucks, doesn't it?"

Taking off work during this testing time never entered my mind. I'm not sure if it was because of my mentality as a business owner or a hairstylist. I would never call in sick unless my children were ill and Bahgat couldn't get home, or my head was in the toilet. Money wasn't an issue, but I was concerned that my clients might go to a new salon if testing took too much time away from my work. Luckily, my sister and fellow stylists accommodated my clients as much as possible, shuffling as many as twenty appointments a day.

I kept myself from losing my sanity by rushing from each traumatic test back to work pretending life was normal. I knew no different way to act; it was my way of surviving the nightmare I found myself in.

Only later would I learn how denial would come back and bite me in the butt.

Chapter 9
Forward—March

The last doctor I saw in this battery of tests was a gynecologist. I was going to need someone skilled at doing rare vaginal reconstruction and he came highly recommended. Bahgat, Mom, and I met the personable doctor with a kind look in his eyes. With his hair, facial features, and gentle voice, he could have been a distant cousin of Bill Clinton. He had a calm and reassuring demeanor as he described the vaginal reconstruction plan. He took out a notepad and drew something resembling a horseshoe.

I wish I were on a beach right now, watching the hypnotic rhythm of the waves after drinking three of those blue Hawaiian drinks with the plastic swords of fresh pineapple.

The doctor rambled on about something.

Make that—nine drinks.

Faintly, in the recesses of my mind, I could hear dialogue among my husband, mother, and the doctor. I wasn't paying attention until my ears perked up at something odd.

What did he say I might have to wear? A dilator? I better focus in on this conversation.

No more avoiding it. I had to tune in now. The gynecologist explained that he would cut my labia in several places and reconstruct them inside my body to make a new vaginal wall. The surgery would be extensive with scar tissue a likely result. The vagina might close completely. Since I was a relatively young married woman and sexually active, a dilator might be necessary to keep the tissues from healing shut.

Without hesitating, I said sarcastically, "If I have to wear a dilator, I hope at least it vibrates."

He laughed quietly and went on to describe how the hysterectomy would bring on early menopause, requiring me to take hormone therapy. He assured me that I should have full sexual capacity again with the help of a lubricant, and in time, a normal sex life. Along with a routine annual gynecology exam, I would have an internal scraping. Since the labia would be tucked inside the vaginal cavity, so would be the hair. Sloughed off pubic hair would get trapped in folds of skin and needed to be removed once a year to prevent odor and infection.

I have hairballs to worry about now? I feel pretty, oh so pretty. If I was going to have reconstruction, why not a simple tummy tuck?

"Should I have surgery, chemo, or radiation first?"

"Surgery must be first. I couldn't do the operation on radiated tissues; they need to be supple. Radiation would reduce their elasticity."

Finally, a decision had been made for me regarding the sequence of treatment; the battle plan is firmly in place. Cancer, you'll soon be history.

"Is there a big need for vaginal reconstruction out there?"

"Thankfully, no."

"How many times have you done this operation?

Quietly he said, "You would be the second woman in eleven years that would require this kind of reconstruction. It was quite successful."

Did I hear him right? I sure hope he hasn't lost his touch. He must be honest anyway. All of a sudden number two has a false sound of comfort to it, but he has a little experience.

"Are there other surgeons in the Twin Cities who have more experience with this surgery?"

Not to his knowledge. He had consulted on other cases, but this was a rare procedure. It seemed the only thing left to do was to schedule the operation. He would call me in a couple of days after the surgeons coordinated their schedules.

I would never be able to make love again with Bahgat quite the same way. Another body part I had taken for granted soon would be gone. It hurt too much to make love now, and I felt sad that we would never be able to experience that familiarity again. Luckily, it wasn't our bodies that held our relationship together.

Chapter 10
Scars and Stripes Forever

Surgery was scheduled for ten a.m. October 24th. I spent time in admissions verifying my current address and insurance provider, and then was escorted to my room on the cancer floor.

We walked into the spotlessly clean room decorated with the pretense of friendliness and comfort. My tone mirrored the false sense of security around me.

"Bahgat, we finally have time away from the kids. Don't you wish we were at a hotel instead of here? Do you think we could get some tea and muffins delivered from room service?"

We sat across from each other in front of the window. Our knees touched, we held hands, but couldn't find the right words to comfort one another.

A few minutes later, a nurse entered the room and introduced himself and asked if I had any questions. I expressed a few concerns about the surgery. With an air of detached efficiency, he launched into his version of a pep talk.

"You are going to have some extensive surgery, but there are many patients on this floor who aren't as fortunate as you. Some of them will not be leaving here. You will make it out of here. Consider yourself one of the lucky ones."

Oh, I'm lucky all right. I'm about to have my rectum removed, my cheeks sewn shut, and my vagina dissected. Not to mention the bag of crap hanging off me for the rest of my life.

"Yeah, you're right," I responded quietly.

As I finished the last of the bowel-cleansing prep solution, my parents came by to stay with Bahgat while I was in surgery. Signing the visitor book Michele had given me, my dad's message reflected my family's uniquely warped thinking, "Stay loose!"

One more thing I had taken for granted. It was convenient. Even saying good-bye to that disagreeable task felt like a loss. I never thought I would miss wiping my butt—until now.

My mother came to my bed with a box in her hand, "This is for you, Brenda."

"Wow, Mom, a gift?"

I quickly opened the box and inside was an exquisite pair of earrings. She rarely gave spontaneous gifts, and I was touched by her gesture.

"They are beautiful, Mom. Thanks."

"There will be another pair waiting for you when you get out of surgery."

"Is this a bribe, Mom? I bet the other pair is even better. You're saving them in case I die, then you'd get to keep the really good ones, right?"

"Oh, Brenda, how can you say that?" she said, shaking her head.

"Now I have a reason to live, if the suspense doesn't kill me," I teased her.

She laughed nervously as she bent down to kiss me.

The time for surgery was getting closer, and I was ready to bolt at any excuse. I was determined to cancel the whole thing if the surgeon walked into my room with little pieces of tissue stuck to his face. When he did show up before surgery, I told him there were a couple hundred people praying for him to do a good job.

The Rear Admiral countered, "I don't care about them, but I do care about your husband and your two little ones waiting for you at home. Everything will be fine, Brenda."

As I lay on the gurney rolling into the elevator toward the surgical suite, I noticed the second surgeon that would be doing my vaginal reconstruction was riding along.

"Do you have steady hands?" I teased.

"Yep, so far I've only had one cup of coffee today" as he showed me his level hands.

"Make my husband happy now, okay?

"How about if I make you both happy?"

I was laughing as I entered the operating room. It was cold, sterile, and brightly lit; my humor disappeared instantly. I wished I had followed Bahgat's suggestion to stick a Post-it note to my derrière that said, "You can all kiss my a— good-bye."

The procedure began: Abdominoperineal resection of the rectum with incontinuity with section of the distal vagina, total abdominal hysterectomy with bilateral salpingo-oophorectomy, incidental appendectomy, descending end colostomy of the colon, and vaginal reconstruction with bulbo cavernosal flaps.

It was easier when I told most people I was sliced, diced, and rearranged.

As my head cleared from seven hours of anesthesia, I was thankful to find myself in a hospital recovery room, gradually realizing that every part of my body hurt. The intensive care unit (ICU) staff asked me to rate my pain on a scale of 1-10 with 10 being the worst.

Is this a trick question? Getting a papercut—1; flu shot—3; pulled muscle—5; dental filling without Novocain—7; labor—8,9; delivery without drugs—10.

I had staples from my chest to my pubic region, layers of sutures where my labia used to be, and a newly reconstructed vaginal wall. Radiation clips had been inserted where my rectum was formerly located, my buttocks were sewed shut, and I had a new permanent hole in my abdomen with my colon protruding from it.

I feel like someone wearing army boots jumped-rope inside me for several hours.

A nasal-gastric (NG) tube from my throat into my stomach, kept me from throwing up, oxygen helped me breathe, and drains removed excess blood. I wore highly fashionable pneumatic boots that gently squeezed air to promote blood circulation in my legs. An automatic blood pressure cuff tightened and loosened on my arm methodically.

The Foley catheter inserted into my bladder collected urine, and intravenous fluids dripped slowly into my body. Patches on my chest to monitor my heart were attached to wires that ran everywhere. I thought I had a high pain tolerance, but I had to tell them it hurt like hell.

"I guess I'd have to rate this a 13."

"Don't worry, we'll be able to give you something to make you comfortable very soon," the nurse assured me.

I guess they have to make sure I live before they can knock me out again. I wish it was two weeks from now and this pain was behind me.

I awoke again to find my husband smiling at me. Bahgat leaned close. I knew he was going to say something special, just the right thing to comfort me.

"Brenda, honey, right now you look like the back of my stereo system."

I couldn't stifle my laughter. It hurt, but it was worth it. It may not have been the most romantic phrase, but my husband's teasing was the best encouragement he could have given me.

I held my abdomen as I told him, "Good one, Bahgat."

I slept most of that day, thankful for strong medication. Each time I awoke, I felt vulnerable and exposed like a tree stripped of its bark. I scanned the room hoping to find a familiar face. Even with the nurse's station just a few feet away, insecurities threatened to consume me. The presence of a loved one lessened my anxieties.

The next day, my first attempt at standing after surgery was a tremendous challenge. It was an important task that promoted blood circulation and faster healing, but I was terrified of the pain.

God, give me strength to handle this pain, or I'm afraid the nurses will be learning some new vocabulary today.

Two nurses and Bahgat assisted me as I struggled to stand. My goals were simple; keep my head up to prevent myself from fainting and remain vertical.

My eyes are twirling out of their sockets. Look up. Get those eyes up.

"You can do it, just a little more," the nurses would encourage.

"It is vital for you to be up and walking soon after surgery. We want to prevent blood clots."

The following day when I couldn't convince myself to get going, a nurse shared her personal struggle with multiple sclerosis.

"Some days are harder to get started than others, but I do it anyway. You must do the same."

She is strong. I want to be like her. Who am I to complain? My stitches will mend; my body will heal.

With Bahgat lending support again, I took a couple of steps and received lots of praise for the effort. The nurses laughed with me at my bed hair, especially when they found out I had been a hair stylist for twenty years. They rewarded my walking accomplishment by shampooing my hair, teasing me mercilessly.

"If your customers could only see you now, they might run away. Maybe we should take one of those before and after pictures."

Without hesitation I retorted, "Better put on the smoky lens and only from the neck up."

My right has been rolled up.
My left has been driven back.
My center has been smashed.
I have ordered an advance
from all directions.

—Attributed to General Foch, World War I

*F*ive days in ICU passed in a haze of faces in uniform, blood pressure checks, needle pokes, and X-rays. When I moved to the regular floor, the amount of attention I got from the nursing staff was considerably less. I survived the terrifying ride from the sprinting hospital orderly and was about to be transferred to my new bed.

"I'm worried you're going to drop me," I said to the transfer team.

"Too much paperwork to fill out if we do that," the nurse said with a laugh.

I just started to feel safely tucked into my new surroundings when a bedraggled nurse entered the room, irked that she had inherited me late in her shift.

"How are you tonight?" I asked in my most charming voice.

She exhaled her contempt and barely glanced my way.

"Busy day today?" I asked.

"I thought my shift was over but apparently not," she snapped.

"I'll try to be gentle with you," I joked.

No amount of lighthearted banter could warm up her cold attitude.

Reluctantly I told her, "The ICU staff told me to remind my nurse that the NG tube was clamped and supposed to be pulled in a few hours."

She didn't acknowledge that my lips even moved.

"You can probably read it on my chart," I said as she busied herself with changing my IV bag.

A short time later, the nursing assistant came in to take my blood pressure. Unfamiliar with using the large cuff, he had difficulty getting it to stay tight.

After a couple of attempts, he unabashedly said, "That should be good enough."

"Could you make sure you get an accurate reading? I learned in ICU that significant changes in blood pressure could indicate internal bleeding."

"Really?" he asked with a puzzled look.

This seems like new information to him. I've got to get out of here. These people are going to kill me.

My friend, Michele, was visiting me later when I noticed I was lying in a yellow-green liquid.

"Oh my God, Michele, what do you think this is? Will you look to see if the urine is going into the bag on the side of my bed?"

"It looks like that is working fine; I don't think that's it."

It only took a moment to figure out the NG tube clamp had loosened and bile from my stomach was running onto my bed.

After we pushed the call button, Miss Not-So-Friendly nurse came in, looked over the situation and exclaimed, "No one told me the NG tube had to be removed. We'll change your bedding first and then someone else will be in to pull the tube."

Thank God it won't be her.

Next, I did something that I've never done before. I gave her the finger as she walked out. That was definitely not characteristic of me. The combination of the drugs and the fact that her back was to me gave me a false sense of mean-spirited courage. She didn't see me, but in my exasperation, I felt better, and so did Michele.

Coming out of intensive care, I felt as if I was living in the space between when they pull the pin on the grenade, but haven't let go of it yet. My foxhole was my bed, and from under the covers, my eyes darted back and forth across the room at people coming and going. I was deep in survival mode.

A friendly smile burst from the face of a woman in a floral nursing smock as she entered the room. In contrast to the nurse before her, she left a path of sunshine behind her.

"How are you doing tonight?" she asked in a singsong voice.

"Are you my new nurse?" I blurted out.

"I'm Melanie. The evening shift has just come on, and I will be working with you tonight. Is everything all right?"

"It is, now that you are here. The last nurse had a death wish for me."

Carefully she asked, "What do you mean? What makes you say that?"

Michele and I quickly related our experience. I didn't hold back in telling her what I thought about the sourpuss who preceded her.

"Didn't you know that you could request a different nurse if you don't like the care you are receiving from your assigned nurse? That also applies to doctors and technicians as well."

"No I never knew that was an option. That makes me feel better."

Maybe I will get out of here alive after all.

After that first day my experiences on the surgical floor were mostly positive. The nursing assistants were kind, made small talk, and told occasional jokes. The pulmonary technician, who beat on my chest and back to keep my lungs clear, shared stories about her family while friendly volunteers delivered the newspaper and get-well cards. Bahgat's cousin brought five pounds of caramels, tootsie rolls, and hard candies.

Bargaining tools I can use with the hospital staff. Insert that IV needle on your first try, and a handful of candy is yours. Poke me twice, and you'll be lucky if I let you near the jar.

On my sociable days, I offered my sugary confections to family, friends, and staff. I had the popular house on the block where all the kids hang out to play.

I observed the fast-paced schedules of the nurses and saw how little time they could spend with their patients. Hospital routine had changed drastically since my knee surgeries twenty years earlier. Back then nurses offered nightly back rubs and visited for a while before their shift was over, now paperwork supersedes human interaction.

Memories of stories about patients dialing 911 from their hospital beds came flooding back to me while I waited for someone to replace my beeping morphine cartridge. Responses often took longer during the night.

Where are those nurses? I can see them now, guzzling beer, betting on a hot poker hand, cigarettes dangling from their lips. "Someone's light is on down the hall. Why can't those people sleep through the night? Didn't we double up their medication so we could have an easy night for a change? Whose turn is it to get that one?" They'd snicker as the game's loser did the running for the rest.

One thought replayed in my mind like a monk's chant; *I am in charge of my own recuperation.*

My private room was at the end of the hallway, spacious with a window overlooking other buildings of the hospital campus. Late at night I could see the glow of a light as a nurse attended a patient a few floors below across the courtyard. Like a voyeur, I strained to see what the nurse was doing. Was I hoping I'd hit the jackpot and see the naked butt of an eighty-five-year-old man? More often than not, I'd find myself hoping the person wasn't lonely or in too much pain.

I quickly settled into a routine of nodding off just when a lab technician or nursing assistant would need more blood or to take my temperature. There were brief but multiple physicians' visits. One of the first to visit was the Rear Admiral.

"Good news Brenda. We removed thirteen nodes from around your rectum and it appears none of them had cancer. That should make you more relaxed."

Relaxed is lounging on a deck chair, reading a good book while sipping on anything with one of those little umbrellas in it.

I exhaled for the first time in four weeks. Giddy with relief, I wanted to jump up and kiss him.

Tearfully I said, "That is good news. What about chemo and radiation?"

"Your oncologist will discuss that with you after the pathology report is complete."

Happily, I imagined myself buying groceries, making meatloaf, and giving baths, relishing the monotony of it all. I slept the afternoon away until the phone rang. It was one of Bahgat's co-workers looking for him.

"Hi, how are you doing?" the stranger asked me.

"I'm okay. Thanks for asking."

"I was sorry to hear about Bahgat's father. Is Bahgat around?"

"No. Bahgat's not here right now. What do you mean you're sorry about his father? Is he sick or something?"

He stammered, "I'm sorry. I think Bahgat should tell you."

Bahgat's father Mohamed, a retired salesman, lived in Cairo with his wife. Most of his children and their families lived nearby. Two years previously, at age 69, Mohamed traveled by plane for the first time, bound for a series of adventures in the United States. Speaking no English and with little experience outside his native Egypt, he landed in a state well known for its subzero temperatures and snow-white winters with only the coat on his back. He stayed with us for several months until the progression of his Parkinson's disease required his return to Egypt. Grandpa Mohamed had become a favorite fixture as he teased our children and blended into our lifestyle. He reveled in his first bubble bath as we crowded in the bathroom to see his expression of pure joy.

"Lux Katir," he said. "Lux Katir, the biggest luxury," he giggled repeatedly.

We never told him the truth about the electric garage door opener. Mohamed was fascinated each time the door magically lifted whenever he said, "Open Sesame."

I tried calling Bahgat at home but there was no answer. A short while later he called to check in on me. I told him about his colleague's phone call.

"What did he mean he was sorry about your father?"

Silence on the other end of the phone, I felt scared as I asked,

"Is he really sick again?"

Quietly, Bahgat said, "No."

Then I knew.

"Oh Bahgat, did Mohamed die? Did your father die?"

I was crying as he answered, "Yes."

"When did it happen? Why didn't you tell me?" I sobbed to him.

"I thought you were going through enough already. I'll be there in a little while to tell you about it," he said sadly.

I kept the lights off and cried in the dark. Thinking about never seeing Mohamed again saddened me. I was mad that cancer prevented our trip to Egypt. I wondered how Bahgat would cope with this loss; he had loved his father deeply.

Bahgat entered the room. He'd aged a decade in the last twenty-four hours. Wary of my incisions, I kissed his sad face and held him as close as I dared. I suspected my physical wounds were destined to heal more quickly than Bahgat's emotional scars.

Chapter 12
Send in the Reinforcements

My friends became drug pushers. Sometimes they encouraged me in unusual ways.

"Brenda, have you pushed that morphine button lately? Here, let me help you."

A Walkman-sized box held the morphine cartridge that allowed me to regulate pain medication delivered through my IV. The drug companies must have had an insight to this tendency because the cartridge came with a measured number of doses per hour. Left to my own discretion, or that of my well-intentioned friends, I would have been unable to hold a conversation without totally embarrassing myself.

Morphine helped me relax but it prevented me from focusing. Finally I had time for my favorite pastimes, watching videos and reading, but I couldn't keep my eyes from crossing. Still, drugs were a good trade-off for pain.

Besides the sleep-inducing drugs, the variety of people who visited my room helped me pass the fifteen days in the hospital. I was always glad to see my family or closest friends, although I think it was hard for them to see me. When I winced they jumped up to adjust my pillows and hovered around me like protective parents whose toddler is learning to walk.

Often friends came in pairs; they could talk to each other when I fell asleep in the middle of one of our hot topics of the evening like the high cost of bras. I only allowed my closest girlfriends to see how painful it was for me to get out of bed and the agony of each step taken. With a friend on each side shielding me from harm, we walked slowly down the hall night after night. After exercise time was over, they'd tuck me in my bed and we'd laugh ourselves silly.

Despite being stowed away at the end of the hall, nurses had to stop by on more than one occasion with a gentle admonition to quiet down. On Halloween, Peg Bundy, Rapunzel, and a fallen angel visited me on their way to a party. Sometimes friends came late in the evening and stayed until after midnight.

Our conversations were seldom about the weather. Each good-bye included a kiss, hug, or grasp of hands accompanied by a serving of "I love you" or "Take care." I couldn't hold back my sappy proclamations of love.

Balloons, flowers, cards, and gifts began to fill my room. A dazzling twelve-inch angel was the first to arrive. With her golden gown and serene porcelain smile, she found her place on top of the television to watch over my room. My irreverent lovable brother brought the most talked-about gift.

"Uh, oh, Rick, what have you got there?"

"Something from your past I thought you should have now," he said with a grin on his face.

Much to my delight, he had carried up the eight floors of the hospital, a four-foot tall lawn ornament I had given him as a joke many years before. It was one of those plywood ladies; the kind you find in gardens in the Midwest. She was bent over showing a plump derriere with painted stockings and a colorful print dress. I had to hold a pillow over my stomach as I laughed when I saw he had put a great big circle with a diagonal line across it on top of her rear end.

On finding out I had a diagnosis of cancer of the rectum, he had sent me an unforgettable card with a handwritten note.

"You've made me think of the expressions getting bagged and reamed a new a—hole in a whole other way. Love always, Rick."

Many people came into my room in one day, from housekeeping to x-ray and lab technicians, people familiar to me, others unknown. Visitors were a constant surprise. I wondered how so many people knew that I was in the hospital and why they felt the urgency to visit me. Were they afraid I would die and they would never see me again? One day, a gray-haired lady popped her head in the door and said, "Hi, Brenda."

"Hi."

"You don't know me, do you?" she said.

"I'm sorry, I don't think I do."

"Well it's been some time since we've seen each other. I'm Tim's mom."

The mother of my high school crush? Yah, about twenty-five years, I guess.

"Yes, it's been a little while. Is your son with you?"

"Tim was supposed to meet me but didn't show up. I thought I'd come without him."

"Well, what a surprise," I said, dumbfounded.

Hmmm, she didn't say I hadn't changed a bit.

We made small talk for a while before Tim came and soon I was falling asleep again. They took their cue and left.

Another day, a friend's brother came to my room. Figuring he was at the hospital to see someone else, I asked him, "Who's in the hospital that you came to visit?"

He blushed and said, "You, Brenda."

I was in awe that people would take the time and energy to visit me.

In my drug-induced paranoid state, I figured the reason visitors came was curiosity about seeing a person with no rectum. Usually shy in terms of showing off my body, the drugs loosened my inhibitions and I would give show and tell sessions to almost anyone who portrayed the slightest interest in seeing my colostomy.

Before Bahgat brought the kids to visit, I mustered the energy to fix my hair, put on make-up and psyche myself into feeling perky. Once they arrived, I tried to make the experience like a field trip. Hannah played obliviously with her stuffed animals and ate candy. John was a sensitive child and attuned to abnormal behavior. I knew he couldn't be fooled entirely.

"What is that Mom?"

"That's an IV that brings me medicine to make me feel better."

"Does it hurt?" he asked wide-eyed.

"No, but I have to be careful so I don't knock it out of place. That's why I can't hold you very well. I have a sore tummy too. You and Hannah can't crawl on me for a while. Okay?"

"Okay," he said quietly.

"Oh gross, what's this?" he asked, pointing to the bag collecting urine at the side of the bed.

"Right now I can't pee in the toilet so it takes it out of me automatically. Isn't that cool?"

"Mom, are you going to die?" he asked while zooming his toy motorcycle across my bed.

"Well, John, I am going to die someday but hopefully not until I am an old lady like great-grandma. I had an owie that the doctors had to take out of me. I have to stay in the hospital to rest for a while and then I'll come home and spend lots of time with you. You don't have to worry."

Chapter 13
The One Finger Salute

After a week on the surgical floor, the gynecologist came by to check his work. His examination would determine if I would have to wear a dilator in order to have sex again. As I braced myself, he gently inserted his finger through layers of sutures that lined my vaginal area. The doctor explored for a moment and removed his finger carefully.

He held up his finger like he was testing the wind and said, "I had my whole finger in there. All the flaps are holding beautifully. It seems as though every stitch is still in place. It couldn't look better."

"Way to go, Doc, good job."

Thank God I won't need a dilator.

After he left I talked to my favorite nurse, Kristi, "The doctor was just here. He put his whole finger in my new vagina."

"Well, I hope he kissed you first!" She said with a wink.

The doctor gave instructions for me to have a full bed bath. My sliced and diced body presented a challenge to the nursing staff. The extent of my reconstructive surgery left them with few standard operating procedures. The nursing assistant whom I had nicknamed "Mom" began my sponge bath. She hesitated as she approached the sutures in my vaginal area. Looking at the long row of staples that held my abdomen together, I imagined how intimidating it looked below.

"Am I stapled down there too? I'm scared the washcloth will snag on a staple."

"No I don't think so but I'll call a nurse in to get an opinion," she assured me.

A nurse joined her and with puzzled looks, they assessed the situation.

I must be a hellish mess in there to warrant two nurses staring at me. I hope the doctor was right and that everything will be okay.

They called a third nurse to confer and studied me objectively like a mathematical equation to be solved.

Thank God you approach me so clinically. Don't say a compassionate word about this personal place of mine. Treat it like a wound and don't approach me in a personal manner. I can't share with you the intimacy that this place has been for me, and I'm so damn scared of losing it. Miracles happened in this place; children conceived and delivered and love was made over and over again.

My body was adjusting to so much I didn't have time to worry about my new colostomy. The ET (enterstomal therapy) nurse who came to teach me about changing my colostomy pouch did not get an enthusiastic student. There was very little discharge in the bag because my bowels were still "sleepy" from surgery. I tried to ignore her lesson as much as possible, but periodically I glimpsed the clear plastic bag hanging on me. Knowing I had to deal with it for the rest of my life, I wasn't in a hurry to get started.

Late one night my colon experienced regular bowel activity. It was three thirty A.M. and very quiet on the floor when an incredible nurse entered the room. She was a gift, with her calm manner and soothing voice.

"I noticed your light was on. Can I help you with something?" she asked.

"I guess it's time I face dealing with my colostomy. Up to this point, I've been ignoring it, but now I'm afraid it's unavoidable. There is a lot of stool in my bag. Do you have time to review the procedure with me now?"

"Sure. Let me go finish something that should take only a minute. I'll come back with supplies and we'll get started."

This is going to be a drag.

She returned and switched on the overhead light. Everything in the room and down the hall was completely dark. My colostomy was in the spotlight now.

"First we'll start by cleaning your skin. I'll wipe this part and you can do that area."

"I'm sorry you had to get stuck doing this with me. You probably hate this part of your job."

"Actually I don't mind it at all. I don't take care of colostomies very much anymore. There are some nurses on the floor that are trained for working specifically with ostomies."

"I think it would be gross doing this work most of the time."

"I think they get used to it. I remember one nurse saying she was so adept at ostomies she thought she could change a pouch with one hand while eating popcorn with the other."

"That's taking comfortable to the extreme."

Next she showed me where to cut the pouch and apply the paste to seal it properly. My hand shook as I cut the pouch to fit my stoma. Nausea and sweat battled for my attention.

"Over time, it will seem as natural to change your colostomy pouch as it does your pierced earrings. It'll just take a little longer."

There is nothing natural about seeing poop come out of your stomach.

She watched me and offered helpful tips. After I was finished, she gave me a little hug.

"It won't always be this scary, Brenda. It'll get easier every time. You'll see."

We celebrated by giving me the first shower I had in ten days. I still wasn't walking well; it hurt too much to stand up straight. My muscles felt like they had been pulled and stretched like taffy. Using a commode chair with an open seat, the nurse wheeled me down the hall to the shower room. I sat in the shower chair naked, exposed, and vulnerable. Tears of relief spilled while this kind woman washed my back. Thankfully, she left me alone for a few minutes.

As the water washed over me, I realized I didn't have to care for anyone else but me. No one would be walking in on me. No one would be taking blood or vital signs. No meals would be delivered or visitors coming by. I had the unrushed luxury of tears mixed with the warmth of the water. I felt every drop hit my skin. For the first time since I entered the hospital, I let myself feel whatever I wanted to feel. Tears of grief followed as I examined my scarred, pieced-together body.

These are my battle scars. This is the uniform I can never remove.

I had healed from past surgeries, but looking at the enormity of the latest incisions, I knew recovery would take awhile. I acknowledged to myself that this had never been a beautiful body, but it was all I had and I was grateful.

Chapter 14
To Pee or Not to Pee

"You've got to do it, Brenda," the nurse encouraged sternly. The day finally arrived when I would be released from the hospital. All I had left to do was urinate.

"I'm trying," I said, feeling like a five-year-old.

They had removed my catheter and surgical drainage tubes. At last I was released from the irksome IV pole that had squeaked along the hall with me the last fourteen days. Clipboard in hand, the nurse continued talking. I tried to focus on my bladder as I stared at the patterned tiles of the bathroom floor.

"Here are your discharge papers all ready to go, as soon as *you* go that is," Kristi said with a wicked laugh.

"Easier said than done apparently."

After twenty minutes of frustration, I left the bathroom and started the slow, consuming job of getting dressed.

I hope I packed loose underwear. Lift one foot, now the other. Good, no snags on the staples. Blouse, skirt, take a breath. Wipe sweat off forehead. Forget socks, slip on shoes. Stand up, almost straight. I'm exhausted. Stop shaking. Mascara, brush hair, look in mirror. Hey—not bad for a rectum-free broad.

The nurse popped her head in, "I see you got dressed, you look like you're ready to go home. Any luck yet?"

"I tried, but the well seems to have run dry."

"I doubt that, you need to keep trying."

My favorite nurse was starting to annoy me. Even though my body had gone through a lot, the simple act of peeing seemed like a refreshingly normal thing to do. I made several attempts and yet nothing "normal" was happening. I sat on the toilet imagining my goodbyes to the nurses. I felt simultaneously liberated and scared at the thought of taking care of myself.

"Brenda, you can't leave the hospital until you go. Have you tried the water trick?"

"Yes, I even put my hands in the sink for a few minutes. Nothing has happened so far."

"We might have to put the catheter in again if you can't go," she said in a threatening tone. "Keep trying."

Just then my brother stopped by to say "hi."

"I want to go home, Rick, but they won't let me leave until I pee. I want to hold my kids and sit in my own comfortable chair," I yelled from the bathroom.

Finally, with the intensity of Niagara Falls, I burst forth—with an unsatisfying trickle.

Disappointing for me, but good enough for the nurse, "Congratulations, Brenda, you're outta here!"

My reward had come; I was finally going home.

When I was young, I had a red-haired boyfriend who broke my heart. For a long time after that, every red-haired man I saw triggered a memory of him. The same thing happened with cancer and its "accessories." I wore my favorite dress home from the hospital, an Aztec print with bright colors and soft material. I came to associate the dress with my fear of leaving the safety of the nurses and my morphine cartridge. I couldn't wear that dress again.

On the day of my diagnosis, I wore a purple shirt with gold buttons and loose fitting pants. I liked that outfit, but after that day at the clinic, I never wanted to put it on. The simple act of giving away my clothes brought immediate gratification and gave me strength. I finally had control over something that was connected to cancer.

Once home, with the exception of doctors' visits, I didn't go anywhere. I started the obligatory task of writing thank you notes when Sherry called to say she was going to do some holiday shopping and invited me to come. I talked myself into the energy it would require and went along.

I sat in the car while she ran into stores. When she was making her last stop I decided to go in with her. Not wanting to walk much, I hovered by the cash registers. As Sherry paid for her items, the cashier complimented me on the oversized bag with hieroglyphic designs I was using as a purse.

"You like it? It's from Egypt."

"I am fascinated by the ancient language and Pharonic times. I just bought a rubber stamp collection with all of the alphabet," she said with enthusiasm.

"You should have my bag. Would you like it?"

"What?—I can't take your bag."

My cancer bag, the one I throw all my medical notes in, to. Even the kids know my cancer bag. Here's my chance to be rid of it.

"Since you like it so much, I want you to have it. You'll do me a favor if you take it from me."

We both laughed as we transferred the contents into one of the store's plastic bags. I was almost out the door when the cashier ran after me.

"I want to give you something. This is my favorite pen. I always bring it to work in case I need it. Please, I want you to take it."

That night I decided to tackle the thank you notes I had delayed writing for too long already. I looked around for a pen and found the one the cashier gave me. Ink and inspiration flowed together and two hours later I was nearly finished writing my notes. It turned out that pen must have had invisible rockets because it jet-propelled across the pages.

Pessimism never won any battle.

—Dwight D. Eisenhower

Chapter 16
At Ease

*I*was getting used to the comfort of my robe and started fantasizing about returning to work wearing my burgundy velour bathrobe and matching slippers. Sherry organized friends to help me at home everyday so Bahgat could resume his normal work schedule.

The first week home I needed assistance getting out of my waterbed. Bahgat would leave for work and a friend would arrive soon after, pull me out of bed, and tend to my children's breakfast. I made my way to the shower where I began a daily ritual of self-absorption. I had come home with staples, sutures, and a drainage tube hanging on me. The bloody tissue around my new colostomy was raw and irritated. My physical recovery did not fall under the category of speedy.

Sitting up brought pressure to the sutures holding my butt together; standing pulled on my stomach and back. If I lay on my left side my colostomy hurt. Disco dancing would have to wait for a while. Bahgat fitted eggshell foam over my chair and ottoman; soon I blossomed into Mae West laying on her chaise lounge. All I needed were bon bons.

My goal each morning was simple. Get dressed and get to the chair two flights down. Once I found a qualifying position, I didn't move until it was necessary. Frequently, that deceptively simple task required two hours.

Though not many people talk about it, there are usually perks that come with illness. Some friends bought me cable TV service for a few months, and I enjoyed watching the old movies. Other friends hired a cleaning service to take care of my home; a great stress reliever. I learned a lot from watching friends interact with my children. Seeing my middle-aged friend, Monica, crawling on the floor barking like a dog humored me as well as my kids. Mary, a mom with two children of her own, played zoo as they took out stuffed animals and created cages with over-turned chairs. Sherry kept Hannah and John busy with games, art projects, and making cookies. My children formed lasting bonds with my adult friends, and I learned creative ways to play.

Pat, a former roommate and grade school friend, organized meals to be delivered from the church friends every other day for a month and they often included little toys for the kids. The homemade meals got Bahgat through the tough times. He was in casserole heaven and became almost tearful when I told him I was getting better and it was time for the delivered cherished meals to cease.

If a person has a Holy time in their lives, this had to be mine; any day I expected a halo to appear. The mail would bring cards filled with heart-warming messages and prayers that comforted me. Many notes relayed that their church groups prayed for me. Masses and novenas were offered, the Bible study group prayed for my surgeons, and one of my seventy-five-year-old clients, brought Holy water from Lourdes, suggesting I put a few drops in the bath.

"Brenda, it might help your tush, what have you got to lose?"

A coworker told me she hadn't prayed for years, but when she found out I had cancer she asked God for healing prayers for me. Others lifted me spiritually; I reflected on perhaps there was a higher purpose for the experiences I endured.

One of my sisters thought it was not that at all, but that bad things just happen. I found comfort in my faith and it pacified me to think of bigger lessons to be learned.

Sometimes the insights escaped me temporarily as I dealt with my bodily wastes. A church friend came to visit me at home on a day I had leaking problems and trouble with my colostomy bag staying attached.

"Rita, today I don't like living with a bag of s—t hanging on me. It really sucks that I have to put up with this for the rest of my life."

It was attitude adjustment time.

Gently she said, "Since you are going to have a colostomy for the rest of your life, maybe you could make friends with it. First off, I suggest you quit calling it a bag of s—t and give it a good name."

She's cracking up here. Name my stoma. What? Tom, Dick, Harry, Peggy Sue?

"Why don't you call it Perry, after St. Peregrine, the cancer saint?"

Oh, of course, St. Peregrine. Why didn't I think of that? This woman was a former nun after all. I didn't want to admit I never could keep my saints straight. What was the use after they dumped Christopher?

Rita placed her hand on my colostomy over my clothing, recited prayers, and left. Her empathetic rubbing however prompted a bag blow out. Another time-consuming clean up session was on my immediate agenda, but somehow I knew I could cope with it.

I walked along a cliff of despair thinking about the radiation and chemo yet to come. At times I was scared I would get sucked into its magnetic pull of misery. More than my physical health, I worried about losing hope and my sense of humor.

Two weeks after I returned from the hospital I visited the Rear Admiral and bombarded him with questions. Not knowing how to handle my questions about chemo and radiation, he called the oncologist located in the same building to set me up for an impromptu consultation. As I waited for the oncologist, the nurse went over the chemotherapy procedure with me and explained more details about the drug I was scheduled to start.

"You sure I won't lose my hair?"

"It may thin out, but most patients don't lose it."

"My hair is the only thing thin about me—I hope it doesn't fall out." I tried to make light of the possibility of hair loss.

She carried on with her oncology foreign language. Radiation would come later after my surgery healed a bit more. Because of the short notice, the oncologist wasn't able to read my full report and said we should wait to see how the healing process was going before further scheduling.

It was five P.M. on Wednesday, the eve of Thanksgiving, when the phone rang.

"I just finished reading your pathology report and have really good news," the oncologist said with excitement.

"What is it?"

"I'm sorry I didn't have the full report read when you came to see me yesterday. On the last page it shows that neither chemo nor radiation will be necessary. The cancer didn't penetrate the striated muscle. Your thirteen lymph nodes came back negative. Treatment protocol indicates that radiation is not required in this situation. And because there was no lymph node involvement, chemo is not warranted either."

"Wow, are you sure?"

"I am quite sure. I wanted to share this good Thanksgiving news with you personally."

"Thank you for calling me. This is a great Thanksgiving. Happy Thanksgiving to you too. Quit working now and go home to your family."

I am relieved but is he sure they got it all? What if there's one cancer cell floating around out there? I've been saved from that miserable experience. I am cancer free.

Energy came to me instantly. The despair and worry was gone. That evening I noticed I had a spring in my step, I rose from my chair with relative ease, and I stood taller than I had for a month.

I am going to make it. This battle is over.

Chapter 17
Inspection

I would wake up in the morning touching my pouch hoping I didn't feel anything but plastic. The stoma, the end of my colon, wasn't ideal because of its concave shape rather than the preferred protruding stoma. Sometimes the stool would gather at the opening, which caused my skin to feel irritated. A stoma that protruded would aid the waste to go down into the pouch.

Desperate for the bag to stay on securely, I used a solution around the stoma that was akin to medical rubber cement.

"Believe it or not, this procedure will only take you a few minutes a couple of times a week. It will become as routine as changing your earrings," I recalled the ET nurse telling me on a visit.

Because of diarrhea caused by medications and skin irritations around my stoma, I changed my pouch every day and sometimes twice a day.

"Do you want the TV?" Bahgat would tease when he saw me heading for the bathroom.

Ripping off the adhesive residue of the pouch felt like tweezing my eyebrows in slow motion.

The next week I sat with my pants down and my abdomen exposed at the ET's office. We were always trying to figure out something next to use to help in my search for healthy skin. I had visited the ET and surgeon so often I didn't bother using the blue tissue cover anymore; efficiency won over modesty.

"I think it's starting to look better," the Rear Admiral said as he came through the door, eyes locked on my stoma and the surrounding tissue.

"Hello—no handshake or hi? I'm more than a stoma, I hope."

Blushing, the Rear Admiral quickly took my hand, "I'm sorry, Brenda, how are you?"

Often surgeons have a reputation for staying aloof from their patients. He eventually warmed up to me because I teased him mercilessly. He could have had the personality of a garden hose and still would have earned my respect. The Rear Admiral saved my life.

Chapter 18
Is Today a Mascara Day?

As part of my morning ritual, I consulted my emotional gauge before I planned out my mascara usage. I wasn't always accurate in predicting if this would be a day I'd end up crying it off.

One day my father came to visit, and we were laughing about how my living room was starting to look like a mortuary with all the lilies and carnations. The next minute I was crying, and I couldn't explain why.

"I don't know what's wrong with me, Dad. I'm not really sad. I feel okay."

"It's the drugs, Brenda. Your emotions go up and down because of them. When I was in the hospital with my back surgery, the same thing would happen to me."

Knowing that about my big, strong Dad calmed me down.

"Well, now that I've had my cry today, I guess that's out of the way, so I can put my mascara on," I said as I laughed.

Corinne came to visit later that afternoon, I felt good talking with her. After awhile, a foul odor pervaded my nose as we visited.

"Excuse me for a few minutes, Corinne, I've got to check on something."

I went to the bathroom and unzipped my pants.

S—t. I just spent thirty minutes changing my pouch.

As I stood in the bathroom, the colostomy bag practically slid off. Stool got on my hands, clothes, and the vanity. Exhausted and frustrated, I screamed for Bahgat. Corinne came running, too, as I cried, "I don't know what to do."

"Get in the bathtub and take off your clothes," Bahgat commanded.

Corinne hovered nearby.

"It's okay Corinne, Bahgat can take care of me."

I had long envied her body since our younger days in school, and I didn't want her to see me at my worst.

"Oh that's silly, Brenda; I'm helping you," she said as she peeled off her outer shirt.

She talked on, oblivious or overlooking my discomfort. "I have always wondered if I would have made a good nurse."

"I'll take your clothes down to the wash. Corinne can rinse you off, and then I think you should take a bath," said nurse Bahgat.

I felt shy and awkward but grateful enough for Corinne's assistance to not dwell on my life long insecurities about my body.

"I'm scared, Bahgat. I don't want to sit down in the tub. Won't the surface be too hard? What if I slip?"

"You'll be fine, I'll be right back."

I caught a glimpse of my mutilated body in the bathroom mirror.

I look like I was cut in half and sewn back together.

"Could I look much worse, Corinne?"

"Brenda, you're amazing with all you've been through," said Corinne.

Bahgat supported me and held me securely in his arms as he helped me lay down in the tub.

He had great strength and his voice reassured me.

"I've got you, Brenda. I won't drop you."

Once I was in the bathtub and felt the warm water begin to cover me I finally relaxed.

Bahgat continued to hold me, and Corinne tackled cleaning around my stoma.

"I'm going to clean this mess around your opening; it looks like a lot of paste build up."

"I think you're taking this nursing thing a little too seriously, Corinne."

She laughed and gently began cleaning with a soft washcloth. Stool continued to seep from the stoma and she wiped it away matter-of-factly as if it was glue leaking from the never-ending Elmer's Glue bottle in grade school. I was ready to award her a nursing diploma on the spot.

Bahgat knelt at the side of the tub wrapping his arm around my shoulders, while tenderly wiping away my teardrops. The love I felt for my friend and my husband at that moment was bottomless. I needed that care almost as much as I needed breath. Humbled by this intimate baptism, mascara trickled down my face, salted by my nonstop tears.

*F*our weeks after my surgery I woke up from an afternoon nap with pain shooting down my arm. I rubbed vigorously figuring it was still asleep. My arm was extremely uncomfortable, and I kept trying to move it around, thinking maybe it was a pinched nerve from sleeping in an awkward position on the couch. As each moment passed it seemed as though the pain got more intense. I started pacing back and forth wondering what I should do next to alleviate the misery.

My friend, Pat, arrived and I felt relieved because she was a nurse and could advise me on what to do. She listened patiently as my tone became more hysterical, and I paced back and forth across the room,

"I just want to cut my arm off right now. This is much worse than my surgery pain. This is unbearable. I want to cut off my arm."

"You would cut your arm off?" she asked.

"If I had a chainsaw right now, I might be tempted."

"That doesn't sound normal, Brenda. You better call your doctor."

I took her advice and called the clinic. They were concerned that perhaps I was having a heart attack and instructed me to get there immediately. My doctor examined me as soon as I arrived. Everything looked normal. He wondered if I had a dislocated shoulder but ruled it out as the problem.

He said, "I am going to prescribe some medicine for you."

I could feel myself relaxing a little. I felt safer being at the doctor's office. Something would be done for me at last.

I asked, "What kind of medicine is it?"

"Valium. I think you are overly anxious. This will help you relax."

"Do you think I am imagining this pain?" I asked, trying to control my outrage.

No," he responded. "I think you might have had a panic attack."

How could I be having a panic attack? I'm not the type. After what I have been through? I thought you couldn't breathe when you had a panic attack. This whole thing is ridiculous. Why would I be having a panic attack now? I'm doing okay.

"I have checked your shoulder and done an electrocardiogram to see if you were having a heart attack and can find nothing wrong. Your symptoms look like a typical post operative panic attack."

I want to get out of here. This is embarrassing. Strangely enough I do feel better. I'll just take my Valium and be on my way. At least my arm doesn't hurt much anymore.

Within two days the pain in my arm was completely gone, and I started to believe it was possible I had experienced a panic attack. I began to realize how vulnerable my body was, both physically and emotionally, and how connected those aspects were to each other.

Meanwhile, the battle continued over the deteriorated skin around my stoma. I tried everything the professionals had suggested, without producing good results. Now it was time to follow my own intuition. Isolated in my bedroom for two days, I left my skin exposed like a baby dealing with diaper rash. The physical clues or feeling of peristalsis experienced by most people just prior to a bowel movement are absent in those with a colostomy, which kept me preoccupied with my task. It proved to be a turning point for healing and made the tedium worthwhile.

Although monotonous, it made time for introspection.

How could my life be better? What had I been putting off that I wanted to do? How could I arrange my work schedule to be home with my children even more often?

Then tougher realizations hit me.

What if I'm not going to live the long life I took for granted or see my children grow into adulthood? I must live each hour with choice, not happenstance.

Soon after, a wound opened where my rectum had been removed. Difficult to treat myself, the Rear Admiral sent a home health care nurse twice a week. On her first visit, she took the usual medical information before the wound was examined. That was the only time we spent face to face. We got into a routine where I'd drop my pants, and she'd begin the procedure of removing granulated tissue formed prematurely. This would help the lesion heal from the inside out. The procedure was not painful and never took long.

"Hi, come in, you're here to see my best side today?" I would tease, trying to cover up my awkward position.

"How are you?" she'd ask.

I was always "Fine."

Face down on the bed, I'd muffle, "Getting cold out there, huh?"

Our conversations weren't long enough to exchange recipes. I coped through joking and forced friendliness for the three months it took to mend. I never got used to strangers looking at my naked butt.

Chapter 20
R & R

F riends offered us the use of their Florida condominium for what would become our lovemaking reunion. It would be five days alone, without the children, or anyone else. We were excited to get away. The day before we were to get on the plane, I broke my toe, which was a minor inconvenience in the big picture of my health. Walking along the beach had lost its appeal, but I still looked forward to time alone with Bahgat. Sitting in one position during the three-hour flight from Minneapolis to Fort Meyers challenged me, and ironically, my toe bothered me more than my other conditions.

Our friends' home was light and airy, white counters, furniture, and flooring. It was definitely not the place for our small children with their messy fingers, but it was inviting to us. A subtle southwest décor, with calming pastels throughout the condo added to its tranquility.

Every morning a nine-inch high owl sat in the tree and greeted us outside our window. Our friends had mentioned the unofficial condominium mascot "Oliver" might appear during the day rather than at night. They joked about him being a confused owl. He was a Burrowing owl and not supposed to be out in the daylight; especially sitting in a tree. They were known to excavate their own burrows and hide in them, but this one defied all normal owl life. As I passed from one room to another, Oliver twisted his head in synchronization with my movements. It felt funny being spied upon by an owl, but I enjoyed looking for him every day. I began to relax. The condo was picturesque as it overlooked one of the many canals that led to the Gulf of Mexico.

One of my goals on this trip was to see how my body would respond with my newly re-constructed vagina. The gynecologist had given us the go ahead on intimate relations and the inevitable time had arrived. In spite of it being a romantic trip away from the children, this part was scary and painful. I was frightened of ripping apart, afraid it would have to heal again. I was worried that Bahgat would not be able to enjoy our old familiar way of knowing each other. I was the only woman I knew who after six years of marriage and two children, was literally a virgin all over again.

The condo had a large sunken bathtub, which I filled with bubbles to help me to wind down. Bahgat's patience and understanding had been put to the test for months. A full moon mirror image glistened on the canal as the water rippled slowly. Now, loaded with a necessary lubricant, soft music, and a gentle breeze caressing the curtains, Bahgat and I began the steps to get reacquainted. Nervous and shy, I cried with relief when everything seemed to work reasonably well. I was grateful to Bahgat for making me feel desirable, and wanted by him. I wondered if the day would come when lovemaking would seem natural again. The five days flew by and we were happy with our accomplishments. It was time to make our lives routine again.

Chapter 21
Irrigation Detail

I knew I was adjusting to life with a colostomy when driving home from a local department store, I realized I hadn't even thought about it for the entire two hours I was shopping. It hinted at the possibility of enjoying activities without the anxiety attached to living with the colostomy; perhaps my life would feel ordinary again.

Irrigation was a procedure the ET nurse told me about as an option for colostomy patients. The process trains the colon to eliminate waste on a regular basis. I made an appointment to learn about it the day we returned from Florida. It had become obvious to me on a boat trip to Key West, that I should explore other options regarding my colostomy. On the boat trip, my pouch would puff up with gas, and I would covertly let air out. Apparently I wasn't discreet enough when a couple near me commented on the bad stench on that part of the boat as they moved to a new area. Had I eaten more beans at lunch we could have had the entire floor on the boat to ourselves. I was sensitive to the odor but I didn't think it permeated away from me. If I could have bottled it, we would've had a non-violent approach to biological warfare.

Soon I was in the ET's office.

"Brenda, I'll be going in the bathroom with you today," she said.

She motioned as she unfolded a chair so I would be facing the toilet.

"Sit here."

She started pulling foreign-looking objects from a box and began explaining how they were used. There was a long hollow plastic tube with a bag at one end and a plastic cone at the other.

"This bag will be filled up to the 8-ounce line with lukewarm water and hung on a hook above your head. It needs to be high enough to force the water into your stoma."

At this point the ET nurse examined my stoma and inserted her gloved little finger into it and with concern said, "Your stoma has shrunk down to less than half the size it was in the hospital; your body is trying to close this hole."

It felt like an unnatural invasion of privacy that took me completely be surprise.

Someone else's finger is being pushed into my colon. This is freaky and bizarre; I never thought she'd do that.

She went on, "You will need to open it up, I'll show you what to do."

How do we do that—get out the pliers? Bahgat, can you find the stoma stretcher in the kitchen drawer? Mine needs just a little more widening.

"I'm hoping you can avoid further surgery by stretching it out with your finger. Don't be surprised if it bleeds a little because you will be breaking some scar tissue for it to widen."

Without delay we began the irrigation procedure. The cone was placed into the opening of my stoma. I slipped an elastic belt around my waist that attached to a plastic sleeve positioned over the end of my colon. With the chair positioned opposite the toilet, the end of the sleeve dangled into it. The water made its way from the bag hanging on the hook through tubing and the cone and into my colon. When the water was finished going in, the cone was removed and almost immediately, my body's waste products from the previous twenty-four hours were expelled.

The force with which the stool came out surprised me. It became apparent that I wouldn't be vacuuming or riding my stationary bike while I did this; I'd be tethered to the toilet.

Hot flashes and cramping followed and she reassured me they'd subside. It was awkward and embarrassing to be in the bathroom with practically a stranger going through this personal experience. Thankfully, the ET nurse was the consummate professional and made it all bearable with her understanding and supervision. After an hour had passed my lesson was complete and I was on my way.

Your mission, Brenda, should you decide to accept it, will be to jam your finger inside your colon every day for at least ten minutes. These instructions will self-destruct in ten-seconds. Mission: gross but not impossible.

My new routine began the next day as I inserted my gloved pinky finger and pushed with all my might. I was only able to get the very tip over the nail into my abdomen. As I counted down the minutes, I held my finger in place to break the scar tissue and stretch out the opening. Each day it bled a little, and after a few weeks, I was able to get my entire finger inside. Even though it was an extremely weird thing to do to myself, it was worth it to avoid having surgery. *Mission accomplished.*

The advantage of irrigating was training the colon to be active only during the procedure. This meant I could return to work and not worry about stool in my pouch. Odors were no longer a problem because my new pouch had a charcoal filter and sound muffler built into it. When gas was expelled, no one else had to know about it.

Although irrigation required an hour every morning, I knew it would work well with my lifestyle. I had a greater sense of confidence working with my clients and accidents became minimal.

I began making my bathroom a sacred place to accommodate my morning ritual. It was the only space in my house where I could escape my small children for a short period. I decided to make it quality time. Bahgat hung a shelf that I filled quickly with stationary, books, magazines, blow dryer, curling iron, and make-up.

I set up a bulletin board with important quotes and reminders written on it and gathered a long-neglected collection of reading material. I wrote a lot, made lists of things to do that rarely got done, and reflected on my daily meditations. I was able to accomplish quite a bit during my "irrigation hour."

Talk about dealing with your crap, I dealt with mine every day, metaphorically and physically. Sometimes the hour flew by as I chatted with a friend on the phone, listened to the radio, or even painted a watercolor picture. I wondered if I could recruit students for a class entitled, "101 Ways to Keep Busy in the Bathroom."

Irrigating first thing in the morning worked best for me; I had less resentment about the time required when I didn't procrastinate. It became as habitual as brushing my teeth; it just took longer. Gradually routine entered my life; this became my new normal.

Chapter 22
Back to Civilian Life

*A*lmost four months after surgery I returned to the salon. My desk was filled with flowers and cards welcoming me back.

"Hi everybody, " I yelled as I walked in to the salon on my first day back to work. I felt like Norm on Cheers while people quipped around me.

"Well, look who's finally showing up at work, " teased one stylist.

"Back so soon? " said another.

"The place sure wasn't the same without you here."

"Yeah, it stayed cleaner," my sister chimed in.

"Now it feels right again," said my partner, Rita. "It's good to have you back."

All day long my customers would comment on how good I looked.

Did they think I was going to look different now that I am rectum free?

The staff had pitched in generously and presented me with a beautiful amethyst sail boat pendant, and had written on the card, *From now on, it's smooth sailing.* There were delicious treats to eat and my first day back was relatively calm. I enjoyed the camaraderie of my coworkers and clients and realized how good it felt to laugh again. The money in my pocket was an added bonus.

"Your sister, Shelly, told me all about your operation. Sure sounds like you went through a lot," said one client after another.

Shelly, my sister and my business partner, had unknowingly made my return trip easier by explaining to my clients details of my surgery while she styled their hair. I thought my clients seemed very considerate or extremely cautious about the subject because no one asked me much. It turned out they knew all they needed to know and maybe more than they ever wanted to know. If anyone remained curious about my colostomy or any aspect of my surgery, I never minded talking about it. I figured if they could ask the question, they could handle the answer.

I chose to work fewer hours and scheduled myself lighter, which was an adjustment for my co-workers. Prior to my illness, they were used to seeing me work hard all the time. A former coworker said I used to live on the edge when it came to my work. I rarely turned anyone away; I somehow managed enough energy to do one more haircut. Darlene, my assistant would shampoo clients, helping to increase my efficiency by allowing me to serve two people simultaneously. It was a stressful fast pace with a fifty-hour work week, including three evenings a week, sometimes until midnight. I competed with myself to see how much I could accomplish along with how much income I could produce. I was proud of the fact I was in the top five percent earning bracket for my profession.

That was then. Now I have to be careful to control my stress level.

After four months away from the frenzied pace, I recognized stress immediately. Prior to surgery, stress was my adrenaline and propelled me through my day. Now I didn't like the anxious feelings I experienced and took steps to control it.

"Shelly, please don't book me like you used to anymore. I don't want to do two clients at a time," I would plead.

It was a change for my colleagues, clients, and me while I tried to forge a less frazzled pace. I tired easily with many lingering physical problems. Self-conscious of using the bathroom, I worried about the odor and time required dealing with my ostomy. I was conscious of having extra supplies and air freshener on hand in case of an accident. I panicked when a client waited longer than ten minutes while I was in the bathroom. I learned to remind myself to slow down.

Brenda, calm down. She will be okay waiting for a few minutes. You are doing the best you can. Drink some water. Take a deep breath. Relax your shoulders. One client at a time. She'll wait for you; don't worry.

Spending time with my kids during my recovery helped me realize how much I yearned for them when I was at work.

It was painful and tore my heart apart when they would cry, "Mommy, stay home and play with us today. Don't go to work."

Even though Bahgat was home with John and Hannah during most of my work hours, part of me wished I could be with them all the time. My husband and I had never had that discussion in our marriage; it was presumed we would both bring home a salary. Hannah was a year old when I bought my current hair salon and prior to that point I had owned my own business for twelve years. Although I had my kids in day care periodically, it was rarely more than fifteen hours a week. I rationalized those hours were acceptable and thought the change of pace would be stimulating and fun for them.

The reduction in my hours brought in considerably less money, which worried Bahgat in the beginning. After a few months our finances balanced out, and I felt grateful to have working hours I could adjust. I rearranged my morning schedule so that we could have breakfast together as a family whenever possible. It was difficult to be inflexible with my clients and, consequently, many remained with my colleagues in the salon. I had to keep letting go of money, ambition, and availability. I still loved my work, and my coworkers and clients, but they would never come first again.

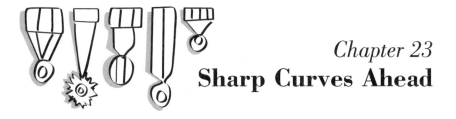

*A*s I began to get better, Bahgat and I had more conflicts. He took life seriously after the death of his father and the cancer experience with me. One day, after a phone call to his family in Egypt, Bahgat was struck with another blow. He found out his mother had suffered a heart attack and died suddenly. No one in his family wanted to add to his already difficult situation, preventing him from learning of her death until three weeks had passed. He hadn't seen his mother for six years, and although Bahgat talked with her by phone monthly, his last memory of his mother was her tear-streaked face as she ran after his departing taxi.

Guilt set in for Bahgat because we were finally having fun on a family vacation when he heard the news. He felt terrible realizing his family in Egypt had been suffering while he was swimming and boating. I tried to comfort him, and I invited friends over to acknowledge his loss. Bahgat turned inward with his grief. His puns disappeared and he was short tempered and sullen. Along with his loss of humor, and childlike sense of fun and spontaneity, he became an even more rigid Mr. Responsible.

I woke up one morning with a vivid analogy from a dream of what our family was enduring through the recent grief.

After Bahgat took my hand and helped me up onto the buckboard and got the kids settled in the back of the uncovered wagon, he hoisted himself into the seat beside me, grabbed the reins, and called "Giddyap." We took off for a ride in the country. I half expected to run into Laura and Charles Ingalls. The team of horses was strong and powerful but Bahgat seemed confident in his ability to control them. Soon the horses sped up, and as Bahgat struggled to hold the reins tighter, I turned to look at the children. They were laughing, oblivious to the dangerous speed as they held each other.

Up ahead I saw a curve nearing. I feared we were going to crash the wagon. I was terrified but tried not to show my kids how scared I was as I grabbed firmly onto Bahgat's arm.

Bahgat was white-knuckling the reins as he drove us through the treacherous turn. Even after our pace slowed, every muscle in his body remained tense while his eyes remained transfixed on the road ahead.

"Good job, Bahgat, you can relax and enjoy the view," I encouraged.

"Looking at the view is a luxury I can not afford right now," he spat out between clenched teeth. "I am busy saving our family."

My words fell on deaf ears. Conversation ceased. The wagon slowed to a stop, and we had entered a peaceful landscape with snow-capped mountains. John, Hannah, and I marveled at eagles flying overhead and the beauty of nature around us. The wagon no longer moved but Bahgat couldn't release the reins.

I talked softly to him. Quietly I encouraged him, "Bahgat— it's time to let go of the reins."

I loved him and he couldn't feel it. I helped him by prying away one finger at a time. It took a long time before the reins fell out of his hands. Finally, I saw him begin to look around. We got off the wagon, looked at each other, and took a breath of the fresh country air.

I told Bahgat about my dream. We talked about how tense our lives had been through the last year and how the dream symbolized a lot of what we felt. Bahgat felt the pressure to support the family and was still dealing with the grief of his parents. We pledged to one another that we were still in this together for the long haul, and that we loved each other. We hoped the time would come again when we could worry about stupid things, like shutting the garage door, or taking off the shoes in the house. We were tired of the stress of health issues, death, and feeling sad.

Bahgat said, "We're in the same boat together, let's start paddling in the same direction. We'll take turns steering—okay?"

"Okay" I said, grateful for the conversation.

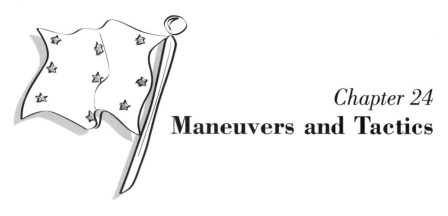

Chapter 24
Maneuvers and Tactics

Consumed with my new physical changes, it became obvious life went on as usual for everyone around me. My world had changed and I couldn't explain it to others. I worried about being self-absorbed, but at the same time, I couldn't stop myself from talking and complaining about my daily physical woes. My perspective was different and would never be the same.

I felt sad about living with a colostomy even though I was grateful for life. I thought of people I knew that were paralyzed and how they probably wished for something as easy as a colostomy to deal with. Often I reprimanded myself.

What am I sad about? What's a rectum, part of a vagina, ovaries, and a uterus? I can walk. I can see. I can hear. I can touch.

Mary, a friend who knew just about everything about me, handed me a brochure.

"Maybe you'd be interested in a place like this. Pathways is a health crisis resource center in Minneapolis that welcomes people coping with life threatening illnesses or chronic health issues free of charge. Volunteers give classes on meditation or individual sessions of massage, and many other alternative therapies."

An angular building with three floors, located in the busy uptown area, became my safe environment to begin the grieving process for the loss of my body parts. The director was a compassionate man that had experienced the death of too many people, but seemed to have endless room in his heart to love more. The walls oozed of acceptance and volunteers handled the diverse medical issues well. An understanding language was spoken at Pathways between the participants, that was as fast as the speed of light. Time was always of the essence.

I began a nine-week class called Renewing Life. Each week I learned to make choices that were better for me. Sometimes that meant looking at relationships, stressful jobs, or simply not getting enough rest. I could see positive changes taking place in learning about the meaning of illness, redefining my life and its purpose.

During class we were taught relaxation techniques. One reflection asked us to visualize our physical bodies sitting in a chair while our essences or souls sat in an opposite chair. The meditation guided us through a conversation between our physical bodies and our souls.

I saw my body as an elongated mound of flesh lacking limbs or facial definition. The seemingly lifeless mass was covered with multiple raw surgical scars. Tears streamed down the front of it. My battered body was exhausted from trying to heal. It begged for rest from further surgeries and had its own language.

Hey Brenda, this has got to stop. I barely get one part healed and you develop another problem. Lucky for you, I'm a fast healer. I'll take care of your physical needs, but enough already. By the way, I don't think you should enter any Mrs. America contests soon.

The shimmering essence that represented my personality and energy sitting in the chair opposite was radiant beyond description. The colors were vivid like an array of miniature lights that glistened like precious gems in a well-lit jewelry display. It moved and sparkled like when Scotty beamed Captain Kirk up on Star Trek. The essence spoke,

Brenda, there is such a dynamic nature within you. Free will, strength, and humor, glitter constantly around you and the calm and creativity of God mingle within.

I meditated on the essence that surrounded the body with tenderness and compassion while declaring,

All will be well. Thank you for your enduring patience and strength of healing.

My body and soul respected each other deeply and understood the importance of each part, to make me complete. Even though it was sentimental, when the exercise was over, I was reminded I was a unique woman like no other in the world, and life was full of gifts to discover.

The two hundred volunteers at Pathways offered a multitude of talents from energy balancing, yoga, art, dance, and drumming. I tried as many services as time allowed; some were familiar, while others challenged my more pragmatic side.

At times during my visits, I found myself thinking:

This is weird, having people humming over me. How does she know about my family from five generations back? What does he mean I need to be more grounded? What does my energy feel like? How come I can't see my aura?

I watched a man push unseen energy toward my body. Another volunteer taught me about my chakras, and I listened as he described visions about me that came to his mind. These unusual talents never scared me. On the contrary, my curiosity about alternative healings was satiated through these experiences. Even though I may not have understood what he or she was trying to accomplish, I was touched by each volunteer's desire to help me. It felt sacred to have care from strangers selflessly giving their time, and I felt the greater good of humanity working in my life. In return I blessed them with my good thoughts.

I cried and healed; we learned to let loose and wail out loud. I began to acknowledge my desire to become a comedian and go to college. It was at Pathways where I discovered my public voice and began to utilize the passion to share my story on a broader level.

For our final class, we were invited to bring someone who had nurtured us through our illness. I limited myself to ten people with Bahgat being my first choice. I had so much to thank him for, and I wanted to do it publicly. I wished I could have brought one hundred friends and family because so many people had helped me along the way. We had the chance to say how each person had affected us and tell them why we appreciated them.

I grabbed his hands in mine, "Bahgat, it has been tough on us, this cancer thing. You have been such a hard working husband, and good dad. I know you love the kids and me because I see how hard you work for us, not only at your job, but around the house as well. Thank you for supporting me in every way you could."

With wet eyes, he said, "You're welcome."

My father and mother tearfully accepted my thanks for their help with the children and my appointments. My friends and my sister, Shelly, let me gush on about them until we were all in tears. The tissues were being passed around the room like appetizers. Some of my fellow participants who had terminal diagnoses shared eloquent declarations of love for their chosen ones. All present felt privileged to witness the powerful testimonies.

I resolved to live in the moment whenever possible. Time was precious and I didn't want to waste a minute of it. Much to my husband's dismay, I was determined to never spend a whole day of my life cleaning my house again. My windows would probably need attention, but not more than my daughter or son. Pathways helped me to clarify how I wanted to live the rest of my life, with purpose, choice, and bold announcements of love. I didn't want to live with regrets. Ironically, cancer became a gift of opportunity that enhanced my life.

Chapter 25
Let's Call the
Whole Thing Off

One day at home with my sister, Amy, she started to gently push me to take action about my aspiration to become a comedian.

"Remember, you said you'd do it for your 40th birthday. You only have six months left; you'd better get started."

"I have been a little preoccupied," I retorted.

Amy's reminder kept gnawing at me and finally I started working toward my comedy goal. Once I became committed to this buried dream, everything seemed to fall in place. Encouraged by my friend, Michele, who kindly typed out my stories, combined with a gift of a comedy class from Mary who knew I would love it; I had the impetus I needed. At last I would begin my long-held desire of becoming a comedian.

Confronting my comedy dream meant I had to face the demons that zapped my self-confidence.

I have no clue how to create a joke, what if writing is really hard to do? Am I smart enough to write great material? What if no one thinks my jokes are funny?

I reflected on what I had lived through these last few months and my wiser internal voice spoke again.

When am I going to do comedy if I don't do it now? What if I humiliate myself? I survived cancer of the rectum. Embarrassing myself in front of a bunch of strangers can't compare. I know I'll have regrets if I don't at least try.

Where once I preferred the status quo, now I was willing to be uncomfortable and make sacrifices to make a dream come true.

In the movie, *Shall We Dance?*, Ginger Rogers and Fred Astaire, sang a song entitled, "Let's Call The Whole Thing Off." They made fun of the unusual way their partner said tomato and potato. I don't think the characters had much of a grasp of diversity if that was tough on them. Bahgat and I must have low expectations. We're thrilled if we don't feel like throwing a tomato at each other! Saying tomato and potato differently is the least of our problems.

Bahgat often wanted me to "call the whole thing off." He had a hard time understanding why a mother of two small children would want to go into nightclubs to perform. From his cultural perspective it was highly unusual.

I wore Bahgat down with my constant haranguing about attending the class. He reluctantly agreed to the time I would need to study comedy. I had a nice dinner ready for him when he came home from work and tried to make it easy as I handed off the kids to pursue this calling. Tired and frustrated with my dreams and the reality of his pressured life, he couldn't resist questioning my choice right before I left the house. It was made more difficult by the kids crying for me to stay home even though I had been with them every moment for the previous four days. I felt exasperated and joyless as I left for the thirty-minute trip to downtown Minneapolis every Monday night.

Instead of rehearsing my routine in the car, I examined every step of my actions. I was confused by the tug-of-war going on within me. I wanted to please Bahgat, be a good mom, and enjoy this time to explore my wishes. I didn't believe this had to be an either/or situation, and I was saddened by the conflict surrounding it. If we had a fight before I left the house, it was difficult to go on stage to make people laugh. It didn't feel genuine. I knew I had to work out something with Bahgat so I could feel better when I left home. It was hard to leave each Monday night knowing he was disgruntled, yet I was afraid if I didn't pursue this goal, I would resent him. I tried to explain my feelings and reluctantly provided him with the words to say to me as I left the house. It became a necessary game between us.

I asked him to say, "Brenda, I want you to go out there and have a good time tonight. Don't worry about the kids or me at home. We'll be fine."

He dutifully complied, "Yeah, Brenda. Have a good time."

I was surprised to find out that I wanted to spend all my spare time writing material and enjoyed the challenge of finding the right wording for a new joke. Being a comic was just the first step on a series of paths I would explore. I wanted to go to college, travel all over the world, learn Spanish, dye my hair a different color, redecorate my house, work half as much, and play unceasingly. I felt an urgency to do all the things I had put off for too long. I became obsessed, but this time rather than focusing on my physical problems, I was fixated on long held dreams and recently uncovered desires. It seemed as if a grandfather clock was chiming in my head, each swing of its pendulum counting out the moments. I woke up in the morning frustrated there were only eighteen hours in the day before I would have to give in to sleep again. There was so much to do. I felt like the rest of my life wouldn't be long enough.

Underlying everything was the ever-present question, if the cancer returned how would I handle it?

Could I die gracefully? How would I let go of these deep cravings within me? How could I make my last months the best they could be for Bahgat, John, and Hannah? How would I say good-bye?

Being raised Catholic; I was taught to be with God in heaven was the ultimate joy. If that were true, why didn't I embrace it and feel calm about letting go of my loved ones and say with confidence, "I am ready to die"? I questioned people I have known that said they were looking forward to the next phase in their existence. The only good thing I could see about death was hopefully reuniting with relatives and friends who had gone before me. I felt bad that being with God wasn't my greatest motivation; I guess I wasn't ready yet.

When Bahgat and I were married, we joked that our lives would never be dull. That remained true, boredom might be a welcome reprieve from our passionate, sometimes-loud, discussions.

Whenever they were bordering on hostile, particularly our theological discussions, he would always say, "The room is filled with angels right now."

That seemed to calm us both down, at least temporarily.

Bahgat had quit making puns; life seemed joyless. With the death of Bahgat's parents, my cancer threat and hospitalizations, and

Bahgat's fear of my death, our marriage was hurting and we sought outside help. A psychologist made several scheduled house calls, and Bahgat and I worked on communicating with each other better. It was tough for much of that year and some of the next.

It was a good thing we didn't have abandonment issues because even our therapist quit coming to our home. He must have thought we were either cured or hopeless. The last thing he said to us before he didn't have time for us anymore was, "Are you two in the same boat?" We knew we were in the same boat but we were rowing against each other, trying to tire the other one out until they quit. Eventually we took turns paddling, and finally developed a rhythm that worked together. It was time to head for shore and stable ground.

It was difficult to realize that while I had gone through this life-changing experience and was beginning to be conscious of what my truest desires and ambitions were, it didn't mean that I could quit my job and go after them with reckless abandon. Some desires had to be postponed for a while.

I focused on what was most important, it wasn't my house, my job, anything I had acquired, or unfulfilled wishes. I loved Bahgat and my kids and wanted a life with them more than anything. Over time our marriage healed along with my scars. There is the old saying, "If you don't have your health, you have nothing." That may be true but I would also add, if you don't have someone to love and the ability to receive love, then sadly, you truly have nothing.

Chapter 26
Operation Joke-Telling

*M*y first time at comedy class I thought I came prepared with forty-five minutes of funny material. I should have never believed my family and friends; it was actually about three. The first two jokes I ever wrote were, "The only thing thin about me—is my hair," and "My sons eyelashes are so long—they get split ends." There was definitely room for improvement.

I learned how to take lengthy stories and reduce them to one-liners with the help of my teacher, comedian, Wild Bill Bauer. A veteran comic, he encouraged the class to write and taught us techniques about timing and tricks to warm up the audience. Bill urged us to figure out our "personas." How would others see us portrayed? What would be our "stage personality"? I couldn't figure out what mine was so I began asking classmates. Only one comedian, Craig, was honest enough to tell me what he thought mine was. Without hesitation he said, "matronly."

Sadly, I took that into consideration. I was hoping he'd use adjectives like cool and hip, even brazen would have been better. Matronly was a big disappointment. I knew matronly—dowdy, prudish, boring, straight-laced, and the opposite of chic. When I looked up matronly in the dictionary, I found the description, while accurate, was limiting. "Dame" fell under the matronly description, at least that had a little spice to it.

There was another woman in the class who was my age. She had been doing comedy six months for much the same reasons as me, for the challenge and fun of it. Sassy, redheaded Rox and I became fast friends. We got into a routine of attending class and then watching the "open microphone" night at the club. It was fun to see first-timers perform. Later we grabbed a bite to eat and dissected the new acts or our own material. During the thirty-minute drive home I thought of potential jokes and what was on my agenda for the next day.

Before I became a cosmetologist, I loved to observe stylists cut hair. I watched as they picked up random pieces of hair and cut away until a new style was revealed. It was art in progress before my eyes. When I learned the mechanics of hairstyling myself, the mystery and intrigue were lost forever. I understood the steps and procedures required for each haircut. Spontaneity had very little to do with it; every move was calculated.

I found comedy to be much the same experience. The romance of the comic performer was gone. I learned the technicalities of a joke and how to develop set ups, punch lines, and tags. I began to understand timing and crowd rap. I recognized the techniques used to warm up the audience. I recognized that what seemed to be off-the-cuff remarks were often times rehearsed and far from fresh. I could see that just like good hairstylists, great comedians made their work look effortless.

Our debut was on amateur night, which happened to be two days after my fortieth birthday. I threw a party for myself and invited one hundred fifty family and friends. There were an equal number of strangers in the audience, and we all had a lot of laughs. I performed ten minutes of material. I started out with jokes about my husband.

"His name is Bahgat, some people find that difficult to say, so he says, "Call me Baggie." One of my friends calls him "Ziplock." I joked about his apartment, "He had the first stereo surround system I ever saw. Bahgat had three stereo systems complete with speakers on three different walls. The only problem he had was finding three friends to push the ABBA tapes at the exact same time."

I continued with the fact that he was a Muslim and I, a Catholic. "We call our children Muslics. They always face east when they say the rosary. They don't eat pork, but they do like to play bingo." Then I talked about being a hairstylist and working at a mortuary where "No one ever complained. Conversation was a little one-sided. And I only had to do the very front."

I went forth with stories of my naive youth. "It was sex education in the Catholic schools, only then it was called 'Holy Family Health Class.' The girls went in one room and the boys in another. The girls watched a movie called, *That Special Time*. We watched a girl riding a horse, swimming, and biking. She looked like she was having so much fun; I couldn't wait to have that special time. After the class, the teacher held up the various products to take home. I waved my hand madly. 'I'll take that box of 48 napkins!' I walked home eight blocks from school with a box of 48 sanitary napkins under my arm. When I walked in the house my Mom said, 'What have you got there?' 'Some special napkins we got at school today. Shall I put them on the table for dinner tonight?' 'No, honey, we'll save them for a more special time.' I continued on. "When I was fifteen years old, a boy asked me a question that I knew I should probably know the answer to, but I had no clue. I thought I'd fake the answer so I wouldn't look like an idiot. He asked, 'Brenda, are you a virgin?' I said, 'Sometimes.' I thought he meant, Are you good, like the Virgin Mary?"

I went on and on; a few minutes felt like an hour. The audience roared with laughter and applauded many times during my routine. Afterward, I felt as if I was at my own wedding reception line again hearing the congratulations of my guests.

Just a few weeks later, Bill and Rox encouraged me to enter the Twin Cities Funniest Person contest held at Acme Comedy Club in Minneapolis. It was a contest for comedians who had never been paid to do comedy. Never expecting to make it past the first round of contestants, I invited lots of friends to enjoy the experience with me. I think we were all surprised when I won the first round. The second round during the following week narrowed the field down from the original one hundred fifty contestants. I found myself in the semi-finals. Bahgat started to believe I had a chance to win the contest and started rallying friends to attend the performances in my support.

I was elated to find myself on stage for the final round of the contest. There were nine judges from the Twin City area, a crowd of three hundred and lots of family and friends present to watch me. After my three-minute routine was over, I ordered a glass of wine and waited as they announced the winner.

"Brenda Elsagher, come on up here, you have won the title of Twin Cities Funniest Person."

I won a thousand dollars grand prize. I told my husband I'd split it with him—so I gave him fifty bucks!

Chapter 27
Sound Reveille

When my alarm went off after only four hours of sleep, I was glad I was going on the radio instead of television that morning. There was a standing invitation by a local radio station for the contest winner to be on the air.

I was thrilled as I listened in my car to the three disc jockeys talking about the Twin Cities Funniest Person contest winner, Brenda Elsagher, arriving soon. I wanted to look around at the other drivers and shout, "Hey everybody, turn your dials to KS95. They're talking about me on the radio!" I hadn't been a faithful listener; I was trying to catch the disc jockeys' names as I drove.

Mary, my most supportive comedy friend, met me in the parking lot. After a five-minute wait, we were escorted in to the station. The deejays welcomed me as if it were an everyday occurrence for me to be on the radio.

This is fun. I can hardly believe I'm sitting here. What jokes should I tell? Do I have any that will be politically offensive? Do I have to be worried about talking about the Catholic, Muslim stuff? What about Bahgat being from a foreign country and doing all those goofy things? Will that be acceptable? I hope I can fit my jokes into the conversation if that's what they want. I sure wish I had a lot more material right now.

They asked me about the contest, other finalists, my family, and where I grew up. Fortunately, I was able to insert a few jokes into the conversation. My siblings told me later that I sounded relaxed and like I was having a good time.

My guest spot on the radio was the beginning of a miniscule media blitz. I was on local television a few times and featured in newspaper and magazine articles. The Minnesota Women's Press voted me a "Newsmaker of the Year." During one interview, a reporter inquired whether I did any public speaking about cancer.

Though I had very little occasion to speak in public and no professional experience, much to my own surprise, I simply said, "Yes. I do."

Next she asked, "What do you call it?"

I answered, "Humor in Crisis."

"May I put your phone number in the paper so people can call you?" she inquired.

"That's fine." I answered calmly while my insides were screaming,

I just lied to that reporter! I don't speak in public! I don't even have a talk that I give! Who am I kidding? I don't know what I'm doing. If I do give a talk it might be obvious that I've never done this before. Oh well, why worry? Who's going to call me anyway?

The phone started ringing the day after the article was printed. I was offered speaking engagements at local churches, health care facilities, and women's groups. I had to make up a talk immediately.

Experience has taught me that sometimes things work out in ways I had not planned. I wondered what was in store for me. I felt I needed comfort and advice at the same time. I decided to turn to the Best Consultant I knew.

Okay God, here You go again pushing me out of my comfort zone. I guess I am not meant to be lazy for even a minute. Just when I am able to take a breath from writing comedy, You want me to start giving speeches? How about if we get together in my kitchen and You help me prioritize my life? Can I really continue with all that I am doing and still add more?

My first talk was for a cancer center. I couldn't have asked for a more comfortable crowd. These were my people. They knew all about life-threatening diseases and the importance of humor in our everyday life. I basically told my story, threw in a few laughs, and I was on my way.

Soon I was trying to fit one or two comedy or speaking engage-ments a month into my busy schedule. I was not a gifted comedian and the only way I would get better at comedy was to keep working at it constantly. I understood the attention comedy writing would require, and I wasn't sure I was that dedicated to it. I envied comedians who seemed to have a natural rapport with their audiences, the kind that resembled good friends laughing heartily together. I doubted I would achieve that kind of comfort in a comedy setting.

Chapter 28
Waiting in the Trenches

*N*ineteen months after my cancer surgery, I was disappointed to be back in the hospital for another operation. My stoma site had become herniated causing the irrigation process to take longer without great results. I learned I would need a stoma revision (new colostomy site) and repair the hernia. I comforted myself with the knowledge that nothing could be as bad as that first operation. The Rear Admiral had explained the necessity to repair the hernia.

"Brenda, your bowel is in danger of constriction and could cause further complications if it isn't taken care of properly."

The surgery was uneventful. A couple of weeks later, I noticed the incision was hard and swollen. A hematoma (blood clot) containing fluid had developed at the incision and had to be looked at in the surgeon's office. Back I went to visit the Rear Admiral.

"I am going to dissipate it by aspirating it," he said as he pulled out a six-inch long needle.

The nurse prepared the area by laying absorbent tissues around me.

"You'll feel a stick but it probably won't hurt much," he said as he inserted the needle into my abdomen.

That does not look good.

Surprisingly, I felt no pain. There was pressure at the incision and the liquid came out at a rapid speed.

The Rear Admiral appeared surprised it took four times to aspirate.

"The extra fluid seems to be out, you should be much more comfortable."

I am comfortable now that you have taken that long needle out of me.

Within a couple of days, the incision was firm. I called the surgeon and we went through the aspirating procedure again. This time, even more liquid came out.

I'm getting tired of this. Why does this weird stuff keep happening to me? I don't feel healthy like I used to, maybe I won't live past my sixties.

In just a few days, the detestable fluid had returned, the Rear Admiral explained the next course of action.

"You will have a drainage tube sewed temporarily into your abdomen which will remove the excess fluid permanently. It will require a trip to the hospital for a simple ten-minute procedure at one-day surgery performed by a doctor that specializes in this area."

True to form, things appeared more complicated once it was viewed on the ultrasound and did not go smoothly. After an hour, followed by consulting with the Rear Admiral via the phone, the doctor proceeded.

"I am afraid you may not get the best results because your hematoma is not a typical fluid mass but has healed with pockets of fluid in a honeycombed effect. Right now the hematoma is the size of a grapefruit. We can reduce that but I am not sure it will be completely effective. Your doctor still wants us to proceed."

One end was stitched into the hematoma and attached to a three-foot tube, which drained into a bag that I could attach to my clothing or my leg with an elastic strap.

I feel pretty, oh so pretty. I have two designer bags hanging off of me.

When the procedure was over, as they wheeled me out, I was looking for my husband. They told me he had gone to the emergency room.

Oh my God. Did he have a heart attack? Things have been so stressful lately. Am I going to lose my husband?

"Why?" I asked as the panic rose up inside me.

"Your daughter was brought in while you were in surgery. Apparently she has a fractured arm."

I was giddy with relief. They must have thought I wasn't a very sympathetic mother, but I knew we could handle a broken arm. I was tired and uncomfortable and wanted to lie down but when I saw my five-year-old daughter, so tiny, and frail in the hospital bed, I just wanted to hold her carefully and comfort her. Hannah's little tears streamed down her face.

"Are you scared, honey?"

She nodded as I gently wrapped my arms around her. She had broken her arm in three places requiring surgery and there would be no operating room available for ten hours.

"You're a brave girl. Sleep now. Mommy will take care of you."

Bahgat had brought in a bed for me so I could lie down to nap when my daughter did, and he took care of both of us. We were all exhausted. The next morning we left the hospital, a wounded pair. Hannah's sad little whimpers were an outward expression of how I felt inside.

Over the next few weeks, I lived with a double bag as best I could, and Hannah dealt with the huge hot pink cast over her arm. The first couple of days we watched movies and let others wait on us. It was two weeks later when we talked about some unusual details about what had happened to Hannah. She was playing in our friends' basement; climbing on some furniture and fell off.

"That must have been very scary for you Hannah. I'm sorry that Dad and I weren't there to help you."

"I was scared and it hurt bad. Then God told me everything would be all right. I felt better after that."

If only I could be as easily and innocently comforted by the words of God.

When I was feeling better, Sherry and I were leaving a comedy show and were walking out of the parking lot when she asked me, "What is that dragging behind you Brenda?"

"Oh, my God." We laughed when we realized my bag had detached from the pin holding it to my pants and was dragging out the bottom behind me.

Another time I was preparing to give a talk at a stroke conference at a hospital. As I put my dress on, I realized I hadn't worn nylons for six weeks, and I was puzzled as to what do to with my extra tubing. Finally I stuffed it all into my pantyhose and decided to wear a loose skirt. It was definitely not a day for control top pantyhose.

After six weeks, the hematoma slowly drained to the size of an orange. It was time to return to the hospital and remove the tube. I would have to live with a bulge the size of an orange indefinitely.

Finally, to be rid of that extra bag. I feel sorry for people that have two pouches permanently. No more worrying about people accidentally bumping into me and pulling out the tube.

I developed a high fever the night the tubing was removed. I experienced chills and sweats and had been cautioned this could happen. I took my temperature and it was 104 degrees. I was advised to get to the emergency room immediately.

When I saw the Rear Admiral I pleaded with the surgeon to delay my hospital stay for twenty-four hours because I had a speech to make the next day.

"Most likely your temperature is high because you have an infection. The hematoma will need to be removed, and we'll get you started on antibiotics right away."

"Removed through surgery?"

He nodded his affirmation.

"What will happen if we delay this? I feel fine."

"You could die of a bacterial infection."

I was put into isolation and an infectious control specialist was called in to figure out what kind of bacteria I had and the best course of action to take. I called a replacement speaker.

After surgery, I felt very comfortable. No major pain. I noticed I could walk to the bathroom and stand almost completely straight. In removing the hematoma, it left a major hole in my abdomen that had to heal from the inside out. It would require cleaning it out at least three times a day in the hospital and two times a day at home. When I wasn't feeling despondent and down about being unhealthy and lamenting internally over my imagined concerns about a shortened life span, I carried on like anyone else. Always when I was going through the healing stage of surgery, I would realize the vulnerability and the strength of my body at the same time.

Although it wasn't painful, it was unnerving to watch the doctor put his fingers inside my abdomen and pull out the packing. Once again, I wanted to stay on the drugs as long as possible. Since I was in isolation, word got out I was not to have visitors, and I actually rested for a change in the hospital. Even the nurses left me alone. I was fairly clear-headed because I was not on strong medications for pain. This allowed me to read or stay awake for an entire movie.

One time when Bahgat was visiting me, he was playing with all the buttons on the bed and making it go up and down.

I was up so high that I was parallel with the television, which hung from the ceiling, and I was just saying to him, "Bahgat, you better get me down. I don't know if we should be doing this."

Just then, the nurse came walking in. Her mouth was hanging open looking at us in disbelief. I felt like I had just been caught cheating on a test in grade school. In the next instant we all burst out laughing. That was the only time I ever left the hospital feeling rested and well fed.

Four women friends volunteered to help with my wound care. The home care nurse had a training session because a protocol of sterilization had to be adhered to by my Florence Nightingales. The awkward location made it difficult to see clearly. Even though there was minor discomfort, it was eerie to see practically a whole four-inch gauze roll fit into the wound. Eventually Bahgat took over that responsibility, and finally, I was able to do it myself. I didn't go to work the first two weeks because infection was too prevalent. That wound required a lot of energy to heal but after four months, I was back to my new normal again.

Chapter 29
Interrogation

*P*eople are like gifts you receive. I collect people and their stories like others collect figurines or baseball cards. While some packages may be elaborately decorated and don't have much inside, others that appear plain may reveal delicate contents. Saying goodbye to a new friend I met at a conference was always awkward and good intentions of keeping in touch were often impossible to follow through.

The enjoyment I received from being a hairstylist for twenty-seven years is because people and their stories are always revealing and new. I can live vicariously through them or remember trips I have experienced as they share theirs with me. When they talk of their engagement or newborn baby, I share in their joy; at the same time I relive my memories of special moments. If I ever were to leave my salon, it would be the people contact I would miss most.

I am fascinated to know about peoples' jobs and what they do for hobbies, where they like to eat or travel, and why they love their spouses. How other people raise their children or hearing about their struggles through life always gives me perspective on my own life.

I was curious about the people who took care of me in the hospital. I wanted to know about the woman who beat on my chest and back during my respiratory sessions. Did she have a family, live in the area, know she was going to grow up to be a respiratory therapist? Anything had to be more interesting then what I was going through at that moment. I had a nurse that refused to tell me her middle name.

"Why won't you tell me? Is it Brunhilda?"

I teased her about it and yet she wouldn't reveal it. I had lovely conversations with the woman who cleaned hospital rooms about the difference living in Minneapolis compared to the small town she came from. A chaplain came to visit one day and he told me about hospital ministry. Another time I talked at length with the infection control specialist about different kinds of bacteria and how they decipher what the patient may be battling.

Mary brought a priest friend of hers to visit me in the hospital. He had experienced major health issues himself. We had a relaxed conversation. It was so calming that we both fell asleep for a while. The visitors to my home filled me with news of their daily lives and it took some of the focus off of me during that time.

That spring after recuperating, I had to buy my son a baseball glove at the store. Since I had not worked much, money was not flowing and neither was my energy.

Baseball is another thing my husband doesn't know about or understand, so when it was time to get John the right equipment, I got the task. A baseball hat, glove, ball, and cleats were required for the team. We were at the local used sporting goods store only a minute when a tousled-haired, disheveled looking man came to help us. He sounded funny and looked a little strange with his mismatched eyes that didn't seem to follow together. Yet he seemed familiar as if I'd had a conversation before with him. As the moments passed I was positive I'd seen him somewhere. It must have been from church, I determined.

He asked if he could help us find something, and soon I realized he knew a lot more about baseball equipment than I did. John kept picking out all the expensive stuff, and the man kept pointing out alternatives that were good too, at half the price. I decided to buy a glove for myself, anticipating the day I'd feel good enough to play catch with my son.

I was grateful for the help he gave us and went to pay for the gloves and shoes.

Jokingly I said to the man at the counter, "That guy back there deserves a raise for guiding us to the right equipment."

The man at the counter said, "What guy?"

"The man back there that was helping us."

Then he looked at me strangely and said, "Ma'am, there's no one back there." He continued, "There's no one here but us."

My eyebrows lifted in question.

"No one has come in, have they?" he asked a co-worker.

The co-worker shook his head. "No."

I paid my money and left.

When I got in the car, I asked John, "Did you see a man helping us?"

He nodded "yes" as he played with his new mitt.

Some people are gifts who can't always be explained.

Chapter 30
Battle Wounds

*M*y comedy and speaking engagements were progressing faster than my body was healing. Sometimes my physical condition took me by surprise. One of the most embarrassing moments I had since my initial surgery happened when I was about to go on stage one evening.

"Here she is, the recent winner of Acme Comedy Company's Twin Cities Funniest Person contest, Brenda Elsagher!" the emcee announced.

Just then I spontaneously wet my pants. I was trapped, I felt like a caged panther pacing anxiously.

Oh my God, what do I do? Can anyone tell? Who can I ask? Just get out there and get it over with.

Luckily my pants were black. I don't even know what jokes I did that night. I kept looking at the people in the audience staring at me. I was paranoid they were talking about me. Embarrassed, I cried afterward to my friend, Mary, and eagerly agreed when she suggested we get the hell out of there.

Why hadn't I been more prepared for that? This kind of thing has happened since my surgery. Why do I allow it to take me by surprise every time? Not again. I will never go without protection. Mary said she didn't notice. That's a relief. I want to go home and never go on stage again.

I drove home after leaving the club thinking about that upsetting moment. I knew I had gone through a lot, and I shouldn't berate myself for this happening. Yet, I kept trying to engage in life as if I was living a completely healthy existence when it was still just out of my grasp. I started to have a pity party for one as I drove.

Am I ever going to be healthy again? Who am I kidding? I was never that healthy in the first place. I have to eat well and exercise. I feel exhausted a lot. What am I trying to prove? I should just quit everything. Why do I push myself so much? Who cares anyway?

I hated that kind of "poor me" indulgence. Once I started acknowledging the hell my body, self-image, and my family had gone through, I began to heal. Ignoring it and pretending it wasn't hard hadn't helped so far. I knew that my spirit needed healing and that would take much longer than my body.

A year after my surgery, I found a tape recorder Michele had given me to use if I ever needed it. I had forgotten I talked into the recorder late one night during my diagnosis and testing period. After listening to the humiliation of the tests on the tape, memories came back to me. They were painful to relive in my mind. I sobbed for forty-five minutes after hearing the confession of pain. The reality of the experience was sinking in on a new level, almost as if I was watching an emotional, touching, made-for-television movie, instead of being in the middle of the crisis. It surprised me that I felt so overwhelmingly miserable. I thought I should be over it; surely enough time had passed. The next two days, I would relive those tests one by one as I did simple tasks: driving, cooking, or holding my daughter. No shortcuts, the sadness had to be felt. Just as suddenly as the grief came, it went away—for a while.

Six months went by and as I listened to a client talk with horror about an invasive procedure she had done, I realized I had the same test done, and I had totally minimized the experience. When I was alone that night driving home from the salon, memory tears flowed again.

My sister, Shelly, had a terrible accident in which her horse reared and fell back on top of her. Her pelvic bones along with ribs and vertebrae were broken. Unable to bear the weight of her body, she would need to be in a wheelchair for two months. The reality of her situation hit her, and she realized she'd need help with the simplest tasks.

Over the phone she asked me, "I just learned I'm going to need help wiping myself. Brenda, how did you handle the humiliation of what you went through?"

In retrospect, I knew she had turned to me for comfort, strength, and understanding. Instead I came across like a witch.

"Shelly, no one wants to wipe your butt. You didn't have to ride that horse. That is a recreational sport, not something you have to do. It's not like you had cancer. I hope you don't plan on riding that horse again."

She was upset by my comments and quickly exited off the phone. I shocked myself with my lack of sensitivity and compassion. Embarrassed by my own actions, I knew I'd have to call her back to apologize but I didn't know what to say. Little did she know that her simple words, "How did you handle the humiliation?" stirred something inside me. I thought I had dealt with my grief. Now, every mortifying moment during those early weeks of my diagnosis came flowing back to me. I felt extremely sad for two days. Whenever I was alone with my thoughts, another distressing memory came back to me.

After two days, I wrote Shelly a letter asking her to forgive me. I realized my outburst at her was because I was scared and sad. Then I answered her question. How did I handle the humiliation? In a two-page letter, I talked about specific incidents during my diagnosis and recovery. I did the best I could with each one. As I wrote to her, I realized I didn't lose my friends and family because I had allowed them to see my vulnerabilities. I didn't lose all my clients because my cancer had inconvenienced their schedules. I told Shelly I loved her, and I would be honored to wipe her butt. As soon as I could I took the letter to the hospital and told her I was sorry.

Time has passed and I've come to understand that grief visits us in waves. I realized I wouldn't die from allowing myself to feel the sadness of the situation. Just as life has a daily ebb and flow, I realized I couldn't heal completely without engaging in grief fully.

The race is not to the swift,
nor the battle to the strong.

—Ecclesiates. 9:11

Chapter 31
Journey Through
the Desert

*I*t was one year after my initial cancer surgery. I found myself at work regretting that I hadn't planned anything special to commemorate the date. A few weeks earlier, my father had called me on October 1st to remind me the next day was one year since I was diagnosed with cancer. Now it was the 24th of October, the one year anniversary of my operation. The previous night, I called Dad to tease him.

"Dad, do you know what day tomorrow is?"

"Somebody's birthday? Your wedding anniversary?" He guessed.

"Nope. Tomorrow will be one year since I last wiped my butt." We both hung up laughing.

My last co-worker was prepared to leave at ten P.M. when she came back into the salon to tell me about two guys playing their bagpipes in the parking lot. I told her to tell them to come in where it was warmer. Two young men dressed in full Scottish regalia from head to toe walked in with their bagpipes in hand.

"I thought you guys might be more comfortable in here. What are you doing in the parking lot?"

"We're hired for a birthday party in an hour and we thought we'd meet to practice."

"Feel free to stay here as long as you like. I just have paper work to do."

"Are you sure? We get pretty loud."

"Absolutely, this is a big place, and I would love the company."

They were practicing a new song, "Amazing Grace."

Some gifts aren't wrapped up with paper. I wanted to share theirs.

"Would you consider driving with me to my parents' house and playing them a song? They only live two miles away. I'll give you a few bucks."

"Sure, why not?"

I picked up the phone and called my parents.

"Hi Mom. Are you and Dad in your pajamas yet? Can I bring a couple of friends over for ten minutes? It's a surprise. When we get there, go in your bedroom until I tell you to come out. No peeking."

We piled in my car and arrived a few minutes later.

When Mom and Dad were settled in their bedroom, I let the guys in to warm up their pipes. After a few minutes, I called my parents out as they began to play the other song they were practicing which happened to be my father's favorite song, "Morning Has Broken."

My parents sat in awe at the men standing before them in their kilts and berets blowing with such volume we thought the walls would crumble. I watched my parents as they enjoyed the music of the bagpipes. It made me laugh out loud, but no one could hear me. After a few songs, and teasing comments from Dad about their kilts, we returned to the salon and the musicians were on their way.

Over the next year I suspected another hernia was developing. I visited my internist and my concerns were confirmed. The Rear Admiral had retired in the preceding months and I met a new surgeon. After my initial meeting with her, she suggested that surgery could be delayed since I wasn't having problems with the irrigation procedure. I wasn't looking forward to another operation.

An ET nurse tried to assuage my fears, "I once worked on a man who had eleven stoma revisions."

"I don't want to compete with the guy," I quickly assured her.

I worried that I would run out of smooth surface on my abdomen since previous stomas had left a slightly cratered effect. A subsequent severe gall bladder attack and impending trip to Egypt changed the urgency for surgery. I didn't want to travel in a foreign country with an uncertain medical future. We decided to play it safe, delay our trip, and schedule the stoma revision, hernia repair, and gall bladder operations simultaneously. I was getting used to having more than one surgery at a time; my husband would call that a good value.

Surgery was successful, healing went smoothly, and six weeks later I was recuperating in Egypt with Bahgat's family. At least this trip, I could make everyone else carry my luggage. I felt like the Queen of the Nile.

Recuperating on my balcony looking over the city of Cairo brought back memories of our last visit to my husband's homeland. We were sight seeing in the upper part of Egypt in a city called Aswan. Among the fascinating sights we wanted to see was a monument called Abu Simbel located on the west bank of the Nile river in the desert about 185 miles away. It was an immense set of ancient temples destined to be swallowed up by Lake Nasser had they not been moved. Through an incredible undertaking, the monument was cut into a thousand blocks, which were transported and reassembled in its current location. After visiting the sight, Bahgat and I took the local bus back to our hotel, a four-hour trip through the desert. I learned on my bus trip that the Sahara stretched from coast to coast across Northern Africa, an expanse comparable in width to the United States.

It was fascinating going through the desert listening to the animated Arabic conversations taking place around me. After a while, I noticed what appeared to be camel carcasses in various stages of decay scattered across the sand. Some appeared merely to be resting complete with hair over their bodies, while others were partially decomposed. The only thing remaining from the majority of fallen camels were piles of bones. I started counting camel remains as far as I could see. There were hundreds. I was curious about the story behind the camels and encouraged my husband to ask the bus driver about them.

Bahgat said in Arabic, "Can you tell us why there are so many camel carcasses across the desert?"

The driver explained to Bahgat and I through Bahgat's translation.

"The camel farmers of Sudan, the country south of Egypt, bring their camels through the desert to sell them in Aswan. It is a long arduous journey with no food, water, or transportation for the camels."

"How long can they last without food or water?" I asked.

"The physical attributes of the animal equip them with the ability to survive hunger and thirst for extended periods of time, even weeks, but sometimes the camel gets tired. Once the camel sits down in the desert, it's almost impossible to get them walking again."

"So they just leave them there to die in the desert?"

"Sadly, the farmer has little choice but to leave the immobile camel behind to save the rest of his herd. His livelihood is dependent on keeping the rest moving."

I started crying. "Bahgat, why don't they get trucks to pick them up or something?"

"They can't afford that, Brenda."

I reflected that cancer and other matters of adversity often resembled a vast desert to get through. No doubt some of us would have to leave precious things behind to survive. Mine was a rectum and a few other parts, for others it may be a breast, a job, a marriage, or some other hardship in life. Like the camel farmer, our very existence depends on us to keep on moving. We rely on medical technology, our families, and friends to help us through our deserts.

I envisioned my kids pushing me from behind and Bahgat pulling to keep me going during the difficult times. I was always plagued by the thought that no matter how hard some tried, or how much support loved ones had medically or emotionally, some would never make it through the cruel desert of cancer. My own gratefulness that I had survived could never measure up to that injustice.

*There was never a place for her
in the ranks of the terrible,
slow army of the cautious.
She ran ahead,
where there were no paths.*

—Dorothy Parker

Chapter 32
Active Duty

I began receiving more requests for speaking engagements and realized performing comedy was getting less appealing. I enjoyed entertaining audiences with my cancer story and stretched myself to do it in a way that wasn't offensive or difficult to hear.

I welcomed the opportunity to speak to new groups. In the beginning I was preoccupied with the quality of my jokes and my ability to decipher appropriate stories. Naturally I made mistakes and learned from my experience. Eventually, I was able to let go of trying to anticipate what the audience might want and trust my instincts. I began to understand universal themes and move away from the story that was all about me. I saw that my experience had affected my family and friends in ways I was only beginning to understand. I wanted to embrace the parts in all of us that share in loss. I enjoyed including stories of encouragement mixed in with educational facts about colon cancer. I wanted to enlighten as well as entertain.

My first test in sharing the challenging subject of colo-rectal cancer came with my Friday morning Bible study. During my recovery in the hospital, I contemplated how I would tell the women who had cooked for me, prayed for me, and gave their time and energy to my family about my experience. After all, it wasn't typical every day conversation in which someone we know has had their rectum removed, a reconstructed vagina, or colostomy. Many of us are knowledgeable about all kinds of surgeries, thanks to television. When we hear someone has had an appendectomy or a wisdom tooth pulled, we generally understand what they're talking about. I knew it would be a challenge, and yet I didn't want to be silenced by shame or the unpleasant topic of having cancer of the rectum.

A loud inner voice called to me, *Brenda, start out your talk by having everyone introduce themselves to one another. When that is done, have them lock eyes with the person next to them and say the word rectum three times.*

I don't know if it was the morphine or the voice of God that directed me, but I didn't question it. I have used this suggestion ever since and it has been an unusual icebreaker to say the least. As you can imagine I have had all sorts of reactions to that request. Frequently, people are shocked, then laugh, or stare at me uncomfortably, and I have to encourage them to say it.

"Please lock eyes with the person next to you and say the word "Rectum" three times—yes, really—go ahead."

They looked at me, probably questioned my sanity, and then proceeded with trepidation. Some even pretended they didn't hear me. The crowd and the setting determined the level of discomfort or hysterics that followed. Generally speaking, nurses plunged right into the task with very little tittering as if I'd just ask them to say the word popcorn. Church people blushed, looked at me with disbelief, and sometimes had a flicker of shock or disgust. I urged them again, and they would smile shyly and get on with my request. Business people usually laughed the loudest, and then dealt with it by getting the job done.

At the close of the exercise, I explained to my audience that saying the word rectum out in the open helps them get over the discomfort of hearing me say it. Without fail, a member of the audience will come up to me after my speech and will describe his or her own experience with colon cancer. Based on what they reveal to me, I see the liberation that comes from saying the "R" word aloud. For some, it's the first time they've spoken of the disease outside of their family.

I have used that approach with every speech I have given with the exception of one. It was an awards dinner for the Minneapolis-St. Paul archdiocese. The many priests and nuns in the audience along with the archbishop intimidated me. I didn't want to risk being offensive.

Everything was going splendidly in my speech when I realized they wouldn't understand some of my jokes unless I told more specific details of the cancer. In midstream I switched tactics, saying that with a diagnosis of cancer, people were always curious about where the tumor was located. I quickly relayed a story I retold from my days at Pathways when I was lamenting that my tumor was located in an inconvenient location. I reminisced how someone else in my group was quick to point out there is no good location for a tumor. That got a little laugh, just enough for me to realize I could tell this crowd before me I had "cancer of the behind."

As soon as I made that comment there was a much bigger laugh than I expected. I said to the crowd that it wasn't that funny. They laughed some more and pointed to the sign language interpreter at my right standing slightly behind me. Apparently when it came to that part of my story, she didn't know how to sign it properly and therefore pointed to my rear end. I teased her. I thought since she was the interpreter she should be pointing at her own butt. That made people laugh even more, and it paved the way for the rest of my jokes.

I was thrilled to be asked to be the speaker for the United Ostomy Association's regional conference. Right in the middle of a crucial part of my talk, six waiters rolled in a huge table filled with two hundred little dishes of ice cream. I saw my audience divert their gaze toward the unwanted distraction. I panicked for a second before I spoke. At that moment I was compelled to say to the waiters, "Hey guys, I don't think it's the right time for ice cream right now. I'm talking about my rectum, or shall I say lack of rectum. Can you hold the ice cream in the freezer for another ten minutes?"

The crowd laughed hysterically as the waiters wheeled the ice cream back out of the room. Then the audience burst into applause. The potential disastrous moment turned into a great moment for everyone present. As Erma Bombeck said, "If you can laugh at it, you can live with it."

Over several summers, I was asked to give keynote speeches at several American Cancer Society's Relay for Life events. The Bloomington, Minnesota, relay is an outdoor event where team members walk a track all night. On the first one I attended I noticed it was bordered by thousands of luminaries dedicated to cancer survivors or those that died in the struggle.

That particular relay raised over $143,000 that night which was used for research to find a cure for cancer. There were over six hundred participants and estimated over one thousand people in the stands to hear the speakers.

That night I did my usual introductions and then offered the audience a challenge.

"Do you all want to make history tonight? Do you want to do something that's never been done before in the United States?"

A resounding "yeaaahhh" came from the crowd. First I had them practice "the wave," the kind of gesture done at sports events when the crowd stands up and waves their arms. After I was satisfied with the practice round, I broke the news to them.

"Now since you have the wave down, I want you to yell the word "rectum" three times loudly as you do the wave."

I had to get my usual opening in some place. They were what comedians call a "warm crowd." They were there to share a common bond, one of past pain and hope for a cure for the future.

From my vantage point, it was fun to see them waving and yelling and really getting into it. Transpired by that group of people, a chill ran up and down my body as I watched all those who'd been touched by cancer. With reckless abandon to silliness, the crowd loved my cancer jokes.

"The morning of my operation the surgeon came into say 'hi.' I had to ask him, 'Doctor, do you think this is really a good day for surgery?'"

"Why?" he asked.

"Because you have little pieces of tissue clinging to your face."

"Actually, he's really respected by his peers, they call him, 'The Rear Admiral'."

"It's not so bad having a colostomy, I just can't find shoes to match my bag."

"I must admit I panicked, when Northwest Airlines came out with that one bag limit."

"For a while I was taking a hormone therapy called Premarin, that's short for pregnant mare urine. No wonder I always felt like eating oatmeal and sugar cubes for breakfast. I noticed I didn't whine anymore; I kind of whinnied. WWWhhhhhere you goin' honey? If my husband suggested a roll in the hay, I just didn't mind."

I went on for thirty minutes and it felt like two.

My uniform had turned into much more than my body. It was not something that anyone else could see, and it was no longer anything I wanted to take off. My medals of honor were optimism, courage, faith, humor, and perseverance. My daily battles would never be over, but how I reacted to them would make a difference. I hoped I could always find something to laugh about.

Even though comedy was the path I took to satisfy my desires, it became a springboard for another. Speaking and writing were gifts that I looked forward to experiencing more. I felt I was being called. Maybe God was dialing the right number after all.

My Hope

*O*ne day, when my children delight me with grandchildren and they are curious enough to ask about my colostomy, I hope I can tell them it was because of a long forgotten disease called cancer.

Fifty Ways to Help a Cancer Patient.

*O*ne night I was jarred awake from a sound sleep. I heard someone yell my name. Brenda, get up and type some more. I had just gone to bed four hours earlier. Surely I must be dreaming. Brenda, wake up! Get up now! I sat up quickly and looked around me, and no one was there but Bahgat snoring beside me. I went to my children's bedrooms and they were both asleep. By now my adrenaline was pumping, and I was wide awake. I went downstairs to the computer and, as fast as my fingers could type, this is what came out. I hope you find it useful.

1. Send a card to let them know you are thinking of them.

2. Visit them at home.

3. Pray for them and their families.

4. Pray with the patient if they want to do that.

5. Bring over a meal or organize meals to be delivered.

6. Pool money with friends and hire a cleaning service.

7. Come over with friends to clean.

8. Play with their children, bake cookies, or take the kids to the park.

9. Call them up to share a joke.

10. Write thank you notes for them, and bring extra notes to leave behind.

11. Lend them music to listen to or videos or DVDs to watch.

12. Read to them, even their mail, if the patient desires.

13. Talk about what they are going through, even the possibility of death.

14. Wash their windows.

15. Scrub their walls.

16. Take shifts staying with them when they are really ill.

17. Bring them groceries, especially easy things to prepare, like sandwich fixings.

18. Cut flowers from your garden and bring them to share.

19. Drive them to their appointments and go in with them to help listen.

20. Donate blood.

21. Give them a book that you loved and inscribe it to them.

22. Play a board game or cards.

23. Make yourself a snack or bring a book to read while the patient sleeps.

24. Fluff their pillows, wash their bedding.

25. Put make up on them or offer to shave them.

26. Style their hair.

27. Do a manicure or pedicure.

28. Massage a part of their body that hurts.

29. Tell them how much you love them.

30. Bring them ice chips.

31. Walk with them in the hospital, house, or down the street.

32. Let them sit in the car and keep you company while you run errands.

33. Make something together—a new recipe, a simple craft.

34. Listen to them.

35. Write them a poem or encourage them to write one.

36. Organize their photos with them.

37. Send them gift certificates for groceries or food to be delivered.

38. Attend their children's school functions if they are unable.

39. Have a "bring a hat" party if they are going to lose their hair.

40. Pick out a wig with them.

41. Be understanding when they are crabby and self-obsessed.

42. Bring birdseed and hang a birdfeeder outside their window.

43. Do their laundry.

44. Balance their checkbook and help them pay their bills on time, if they'll let you.

45. Include them in your church prayer chains.

46. Find ways to nurture their significant others or caregivers.

47. Do necessary car maintenance if they are unable.

48. Bring them stamps.

49. Holiday shop for them and wrap the gifts.

50. Enjoy each other by finding something to laugh about.

The Various Types
of Ostomies

A Colostomy is a surgically created opening into the colon through the abdomen. Its purpose is to allow the stool to bypass a diseased or damaged part of the colon. A colostomy may be made at almost any point along the length of the colon.

When you have a colostomy, stool is no longer eliminated though the anus. Instead, it is eliminated through the colostomy. To construct a colostomy, the surgeon brings part of the colon through the abdominal wall. This new opening on the abdomen is called a stoma.

An ileostomy is a surgically created opening into the small intestine through the abdomen. The purpose of an ileostomy is to allow stool to bypass the colon.

Because of an injury or disease, such as ulcerative colitis or Crohn's Disease, the colon may be surgically removed, along with the rectum and anus. Remember, the colon's main purpose is to absorb water and store stool. Your body can continue to function even without a colon.

When you have an ileostomy, stool is no longer eliminated through the anus. Instead, stool is eliminated through the ileostomy. An ileostomy, like the colostomy, does not have a sphincter muscle, so you have no voluntary control over bowel movements. Instead, you will wear a disposable pouch to collect the stool.

An ileostomy, like the colostomy, may be temporary or permanent, depending on the medical reason for the surgery.

A Urostomy is a surgically created opening usually on the abdomen. A urostomy allows urine to flow out of the body after the bladder has been removed. A urostomy may also be called a urinary diversion.

When a person has a urostomy, urine is no longer eliminated through the urethra. Instead, it is eliminated through the urostomy.

Because a urostomy does not have a sphincter muscle, you have no voluntary control over when to urinate. Instead, you wear a pouch to collect the urine.

Call to Subscribe to the Secure Start Newsletter
It's free and useful information.
1-800-323-4060

Used with permission from Hollister Incorporated

The Role of the Intestine

*T*o understand the role of the intestine, let us follow the path that food takes as it passes through and is digested by the body. Food first enters the body through the mouth, where it is cut into small pieces by the teeth and broken down somewhat by the saliva. The food is then swallowed and passes to the stomach down a long fleshy tube called the esophagus. Stomach muscles and gastric juices act on the food to prepare it for absorption by the blood. After several hours the pulpy mass of food passes into the small intestine, a 20-foot long tube that is folded and packed into the abdominal cavity. More fluids from the liver and pancreas act on the food, further digesting it, extracting the valuable elements from the foods, and passing them into the blood stream.

This small intestine—named not for its length, but for the narrow diameter—is where most digestion takes place. At the end of its processing, all that remains is water and waste material, which then passes into the large intestine, or colon. This portion of the intestine is about five feet long and has a much larger diameter (thus, its name, large intestine). The colon's function is to absorb the water from the waste material, to transport waste through its length, and to store it until it is ready to be expelled from the body through the anus.

Used with permission from Hollister Incorporated

You don't always win your battles,
but it's good to know you fought.

—Marjorie Holmes

Medical Glossary:

Adenocarcinoma: Cancer that begins in cells that line certain internal organs and that have glandular (*secretory*) properties.

Cancer: A malignant tumor of potentially unlimited growth that expands locally by invasion and systemically by metastasis.

Cancer survivor: Anyone currently dealing with or has had cancer.

Chemotherapy: Use of chemical agents in the treatment or control of disease.

Clinical trial: (R*esearch studies*) are used to determine whether new drugs or treatments are both safe and effective. Carefully conducted clinical trials are the fastest and safest way to find treatments that work. New therapies are tested on people only after laboratory and animal studies show promising results.

Colon: The large intestine that extends from the small intestine to the rectum. It is approximately five feet long in adults and is responsible for forming, storing, and expelling waste matter.

Colostomy: A surgical formation of an artificial anus through the abdomen.

Computed Tomography (CT) scan: The X-ray beam moves around the body, taking pictures from different angles. These images are combined by a computer to produce a detailed cross-sectional picture of the inside of the body.

Enterstomal Therapist: Nurses with further education of wound care and ostomies.

Fistula: An abnormal passage from an abscess to the body surface permitting passage of fluids or secretions.

Gall bladder: The gallbladder is a small pear-shaped organ that stores and concentrates bile.

Hemorrhoid: Dilated veins in swollen tissue near anus or within rectum.

Hormone therapy: Medication which might prevent heart disease and osteoarthritis.

Hysterectomy: Surgical removal of the uterus.

Irrigation: To flush (a body part) with a stream of liquid.

JP drain: The Jackson-Pratt (JP) drain is a device used to remove and collect bodily fluids from an open wound.

Lymph nodes: Small areas located along the neck, armpit, and groin that filter bacteria from lymph fluid.

Malignant: Tending to infiltrate, metastasize, and become progressively worse.

Needle Aspiration: The procedure of removing liquid using a needle.

NG (Nasogastric) tube: A plastic tube that is gently inserted into the patients' nostril and into the stomach allowing fluids to be removed.

Oncologist: A physician specializing in the study of tumors.

Oncology: The branch of medicine that deals with tumors, including study of their development, diagnosis, treatment, and prevention.

Ostomates: Anyone who has had a surgical opening made in regards to body elimination.

Ostomy: An operation to create an artificial passage for bodily elimination.

Pneumatic boots: Intermittent pneumatic compression boots; stimulate circulation and reduce the chances of deep venous thromboses for patients who are unable to walk due surgery.

Radiation therapy: Treatment of disease using high-energy radiation such as x-rays.

Radiologist: A physician specializing in a branch of medicine concerned with the use of radiant energy (as Xrays) or radioactive material in the diagnosis and treatment of disease.

Rectum: The lowest section of the large intestine.

Respiratory Therapist: Important members of the health care team, working with medical direction from pulmonologists and physicians working in critical care.

Stoma: An artificial permanent opening especially in the abdominal wall made in surgical procedures.

Tumor: An abnormal benign or malignant mass of tissue that is not inflammatory, arises without obvious cause from cells of preexistent tissue, and possesses no physiologic function.

Vaginal reconstruction: The action taken to reconstruct the vagina after surgery.

Information Resources

American Cancer Society
www.cancer.org

The American Society of Colon and Rectal Surgeons
www.fascrs.org

Colon Cancer Alliance
www.ccalliance.org

Friends of Ostomates Worldwide
www.fowusa.org

Hollister Incorporated
www.hollister.com

National Cancer Institute
www.cancer.gov

National Colon Cancer Alliance
www.nccra.org

Parents of Ostomy Children (POC)
www.uoa.org

Pathways
www.pathwaysminneapolis.org

United Ostomy Association
www.uoa.org

United Ostomy Association of Canada, Inc.
www.ostomycanada.ca

Women's Cancer Resource Center
www.givingvoice.org

Wound, Ostomy, and Continence Nurses Society
www.wocn.org

Brenda Elsagher
www.brendabringsjoy.com

Colon Cancer Fact Sheet

*C*olorectal cancer (commonly referred to as colon cancer) develops in the digestive tract, also referred to as the gastrointestinal or GI tract. The digestive tract processes the food you eat and rids the body of solid waste matter. This cancer usually develops from precancerous changes in the lining of the organs. These growths of tissue into the center of the colon or rectum are called polyps.

- Colorectal cancer is the third most common cancer diagnosed in both men and women in the United States. The American Cancer Society estimates in 2004, about 106,370 new cases of colon cancer (50,400 men and 55,970 women) will be diagnosed.

- Of these new cancer cases, 40,570 new cases of rectal cancer (23,220 men and 17,350 women) will be diagnosed in 2004.

- Colorectal cancer is expected to cause about 56,730 deaths (28,320 men and 28,410 women) during 2004, accounting for about 10% of cancer deaths.

- The death rate from colorectal cancer has been dropping for the past 15 years. There are probably a number of reasons for this. One reason is probably because polyps are found by screening before they can develop into cancers. Also, colorectal cancers are being found earlier when they are easier to cure, and treatments have improved.

Risk Factors

- Age: The risk of colon cancer increases with age. Nearly 90 percent of colon cancer patients are over the age of 50.

- Race: African American men and women are at greater risk for developing and dying from colon cancer than men and women of other racial and ethnic groups.

- Family history: personal or family history of colon cancer or polyps increases the risk of cancer. People with a history of inflammatory bowel disease also may be at greater risk. In addition, there are a number of hereditary conditions that increase the risk of colon cancer, including familial adenomatous polyposis (FAP), hereditary nonpolyposis colorectal cancer (HNPCC), Gardner's syndrome, and Ashkenazi Jewish heritage.

- Use of cigarettes and other tobacco products.
- Physical inactivity.
- Diet: A diet high in animal fats, such as those found in red meat can increase the chances of a person developing colon cancer.

Symptoms

Early colon cancer usually has no symptoms. People with the following symptoms should see their doctor, particularly if they are over 40 years old, or have a personal or family history of the disease:

- A change in bowel habits such as diarrhea, constipation, or narrowing of the stool that lasts for more than a few days.
- A feeling that you need to have a bowel movement that doesn't leave after you do go.
- Bleeding from the rectum or blood in the stool.
- Cramping or gnawing stomach pain.
- Decreased appetite.
- Weakness and fatigue.
- Jaundice (yellow-green color of the skin and white part of the eye.)

Note: *Signs and symptoms of colon cancer typically occur in advanced stages of the disease.*

Testing & Detection

According to the American Cancer Society guidelines for the early detection of colon cancer, starting at age 50, both men and women should follow one of the following testing options:

- Yearly fecal occult blood test (FOBT)

- Flexible sigmoidoscopy every five years
- FOBT and flexible sigmoidoscopy every five years (preferred over either option alone)
- Double-contrast barium enema every five years
- Colonoscopy every five years
- People with a family history should be tested earlier and may need to be tested more often

Common Treatments

Surgery is the most common form of treatment for colon cancer. For cancers that have not spread, it frequently stops the disease.

Chemotherapy, or chemotherapy with radiation treatment, is given before or after surgery to most patients whose cancer has spread extensively into the bowel wall or to the lymph nodes.

- A permanent colostomy (creation of an abdominal opening for elimination of body wastes) is very seldom needed for colon cancer and not often required for rectal cancer.

Survival

- When colon cancers are detected at an early stage and have not spread beyond the colon or rectum, the five-year survival rate is 90 percent.
- There is a 64 percent chance of five-year survival when the cancer has spread only to nearby organs or lymph nodes.
- Once the cancer has spread to parts of the body that are remote or at a distance from the primary tumor, the five-year survival rate is 8 percent.
- For further information contact the American Cancer Society at www.cancer.org
- or 1-800-ACS 2345

About the Author

*P*rofessional speaker, comic and business owner, Brenda Elsagher, weaves in her humor as she takes you on a powerful ride of emotions with her story of dealing with the physical and emotional aspects of cancer.

She takes the taboo subject of colon cancer and educates the reader about everyday life as an ostomate.

The anecdotes she sprinkles in will produce a range of reactions from subtle tears to belly laughter.

Brenda lives with her husband Bahgat, and two children, John and Hannah, in Burnsville, Minnesota.

But now I am return'd,
and that war-thoughts have left
their places vacant, in their rooms come
thronging soft and delicate desires.

William Shakespeare

They Great Gifts too! make

Check your leading book store or use this order form.

To order, copy & send this form, along with payment to:

Brenda Elsagher
13425 Penn Ave. So.
Burnsville, MN 55337

Number of Books:		
Cost per book:	X $14.95	
Shipping & Handling: + $3.00 per book		
TOTAL:		

☐ Check or money order enclosed,
   payable to Brenda Elsagher

☐ Bill my credit card: ☐ Visa   ☐ Mastercard

_____ _____ / _____
Card Number   *Exp. Date*

_____
Name as it appears on card

_____
Signature

_____
Name

_____
Address

_____
City

_____ _____
State   *Zip*

_____
E-mail

Brenda would love to come and speak to your group!
For more information, please visit: **www.brendabringsjoy.com** or call
Brenda at 952-882-0154. or **BMElsagher@aol.com**
Credit card charges will reflect on your statement as purchased from Alpha
Hair Salon, Inc. Allow 2 weeks for delivery.

153